The John Harvard Library

THE NEW BASIS OF
CIVILIZATION

SIMON N. PATTEN

Edited by Daniel M. Fox

THE BELKNAP PRESS OF
HARVARD UNIVERSITY PRESS
CAMBRIDGE, MASSACHUSETTS
1968

CONTENTS

INTRODUCTION

For thousands of years men have feared scarcity; feared that lean years would succeed fat years in the natural course of events. Since Adam and Eve departed the affluent society of Eden, most men have rejected as fantastic the dream that enough goods could be produced to guarantee every human being a subsistence standard of living. These pessimists were much saner than the utopian dreamers who, since the time of the ancient Greeks, have yearned for a Golden Age when men would not have to struggle to survive. Throughout history, lean and fat years have alternated with depressing regularity.

In recent years, however, many tough-minded students of economic and social life have argued that, in America and perhaps Western Europe, men have solved the problems of production. According to this view, propagated by such commentators as John K. Galbraith, David Riesman, and Robert Theobald, scarcity—the struggle to subsist—is being replaced by affluence, abundance, or an age of expanding mass consumption. President Lyndon Johnson, for example, predicated his domestic policy on the assumption that we live in the "midst of abundance"; that men, freed from the" wants of the body," could seek fulfillment of the "needs of the spirit."[1]

A change is occurring in the way practical men view economic reality; a change from the assumption that scarcity is man's lot to the belief that abundance has become the major factor conditioning economic life and social arrangements. The idea of abundance is not, however, susceptible to documentary proof. It is a concept which rests on subjective answers to the question "How much is enough?" Since the idea is subjective, it could not become a useful tool for viewing the world until there was a consensus about the meaning of "enough" that enabled social thinkers to conduct reasoned discussions about the implications of abundance for economic and social life, public policy, and individuals' lives. This consensus has been formulated by economists over the past half century. It defines a potentially abundant society as one in which there is sufficient wealth for every citizen to have a diet which meets the minimum requirements for health set forth by

[1]The theme of abundance had been expounded in numerous books during the past decade. John K. Galbraith, *The Affluent Society* (Boston, 1958) and David Riesman, *Abundance for What?* (New York, 1964) are probably the most widely known. Lyndon Johnson's views are quoted from "Text of the President's Message to Congress on the State of the Union," *New York Times*, January 5, 1965.

experts in the science of nutrition, housing that does not destroy health, sufficient clothing to withstand the rigors of climate, and education to participate in the sophisticated decisions required by a modern industrial economy.

At the turn of the present century, when the idea of a transition from an age of scarcity to an era of abundance was first explored by a few American social scientists, the overwhelming weight of professional and lay opinion in Europe and the United States defended the assumption of scarcity. When Simon Patten articulated his belief that enough goods and services would be produced in the forseeable future to provide every human being with the requisites for survival, he was a lonely forerunner of the present tenuous consensus. Looking back to Patten from the present, it is tempting to itemize the ways in which the experience of the American nation and the history of social science converged in Patten's thought to make him a forerunner. But most American social scientists of Patten's generation did not share his optimism, although they shared the same historical experience and had been exposed to the same education in the social sciences. This essay examines two questions: why Simon Patten expounded the concept half a century before it achieved wide currency and why the concept of a transition to abundance became part of the way a significant number of Americans look at the world.

INTRODUCTION

I

The events of Simon Patten's life enabled him to develop a unique sensitivity to the economic, social, and intellectual currents in American society in the years preceding and following the beginning of the twentieth century. The values and assumptions Patten brought to the study of abundance were formed in two environments: Illinois, where he lived from his birth in 1852 until 1876, and Germany, where he studied at the University of Halle from 1876 to 1879. From his Illinois boyhood, Patten derived a vision of man's capacity to realize his aspirations, respect for hard work and moral restraint, and a high regard for such institutions as the Republican Party and the Presbyterian Church as vehicles for social reform. From Germany, he obtained a vision of an orderly society, increasing its wealth while maintaining active concern for those who suffered in the process of social change, an introduction to ideas and tools with which to analyze the world around him, friends who shared his enthusiasm and encouraged his work, and credentials as a professional economist.[2]

Patten was a member of the most impressive genera-

[2]Full documentation for the account of Patten's life and thought which follows and for my views on the economic and intellectual history of the period can be found in my book, *The Discovery of Abundance: Simon N. Patten and the Transformation of Social Theory* (Ithaca, 1967).

INTRODUCTION

tion of scholars in American history: the group of about one hundred men who studied social science in Germany in the 1870's and, over the next forty years, became the leaders of American education. When Patten and the others of this group—Richard T. Ely, John Bates Clark, and Henry Carter Adams, for example—returned from Germany in the early 1880's, American universities had few courses in the social sciences, and these were taught mainly by amateurs. There were no periodicals devoted to scholarly social science and no standards of professional competence comparable to the journals and standards of Europe. Two decades later, however, the professional machinery of American social science was functioning at a level equivalent, and in some fields superior, to its European counterpart.

In Germany, Patten and his future colleagues were deeply influenced by a group of economists called the Younger Historical School. At Halle, Berlin, Heidelberg, and the other German universities, such scholars as Gustav Schmoller, Adolf Wagner, and Johannes Conrad produced an impressive body of work in the three decades after 1860. These men, who came of age during Germany's industrial and political revolution, were suspicious of the grandiose generalizations of the first generation of historical economists—led by Wilhelm Roscher, Karl Knies, and Lujo Brentano—and were committed to using their knowledge to solve current social problems. Although they were deeply influenced

INTRODUCTION

by Hegelian concepts of historical process and carefully trained in the research methods pioneered by such men as Leopold von Ranke, the Younger Historical School was receptive to the theoretical economics emanating from London and Vienna. Only in the 1880's, after Patten had returned to the United States, did national and scholarly pride combine in the *Methodenstreit*, a dispute between German and Austrian economists which destroyed the fruitful combination of empiricism and theory and pushed German economics out of the mainstream of professional development.

Despite their interest in English economic theories, the Germans' assumptions about human nature and social change contradicted those of David Ricardo and John Stuart Mill. In general, the Englishmen regarded men as rational maximizers of satisfactions, and society as the sum of the human atoms within a particular geographical area. The Germans assumed that society was an organism, more than the sum of its parts, that man's natural mode of action was collective rather than individualistic, and that traditions, feelings, and obscurely perceived longings were the motives of human actions. Unlike the classical economists, the Germans emphasized the potentialities of individuals and institutions and argued that men and society could best be understood in the context of their historical development. Simon Patten rejected organicism and was suspicious of historicism. Under the influence of his teacher, Johannes Conrad, however, he accepted the historical economists' emphasis on the complexity of human nature and the role of group feelings and action in social change.

Although the German economists inspired their American students with zeal for social reform and optimism about the success of planned change, they did not regard state action as the only way to achieve social change. The emphasis of Patten and other Americans on voluntary action was consistent with their German education. The social program of the German economists, *Sozialpolitik*, was less a new ideology than a new method of realizing the traditional ethical goals of Judaeo-Christian morality within the institutional context of any society. To some men, including Simon Patten, the reforms inspired by the Germans and, later, the American Progressives, were the first installments of a much broader scheme of reform. But that broader scheme was never articulated. Social Policy, as conceived by German and American scholars, projected no utopia against which present conditions could be measured.

II

The external events of Patten's career from his return to the United States in 1879 until his death in 1922 are not particularly exciting. Until 1887 Patten, like other academic men of his generation, taught and administered in primary and secondary schools. In 1887, with one book published and several friends already established on university faculties, he was appointed professor of economics at the Wharton School of the University of Pennsylvania—a position he held until his support of anti-war groups caused the Trustees to force his retirement in 1917. At the University, Patten participated actively in academic affairs and took a deep personal interest in his students, who included Walter E. Weyl, later a noted journalist, Frances Perkins, who became the first woman to hold a seat in the Cabinet, Rexford G. Tugwell, economist and public official, and several pioneers in the field of social work, notably Edward T. Devine and William H. Allen. Besides his university duties, Patten produced twenty-two books and several hundred articles for professional and popular journals, played a leading role in efforts to professionalize economics and sociology, and occasionally advised students who entered careers in government or social service. For most of these years he lived alone, devoting most of his time to his work and his students. He married in 1904 but was divorced four years later.

More important for an understanding of Patten's thought, and the history of the concept of abundance, are the social and economic events which he participated in and studied with the insight and professional tools he developed in Germany and the United States. Many Americans of Patten's generation had experienced in

INTRODUCTION

their own lifetimes a transition from poverty to wealth, comfort, and abundance. The mythology of success, broadcast from the press, the pulpit, and schoolbooks fed the reality of economic mobility which, recent scholarship suggests, lagged behind. Simon Patten had grown up amid pioneer conditions on the Illinois prairie and participated in breaking sod, ridding swamps of mosquitoes, and the mechanization of agriculture. By the time he was forty, he was a member of the professional upper-middle class.

Social and economic mobility was mainly a result of the rapidity of American economic development. In the second half of the nineteenth century, the United States became the world's leading producer of many raw materials and manufactured goods. European and American observers were astounded by the pace of American expansion, the westward movement to free and inexpensive land, the rapid increase in the number and size of cities, and the stimulus to industry from consumer demand created by a population growing rapidly from the influx of immigrants. At the same time, the European economy, except for Germany, after unprecedented prosperity in the 1850's and 1860's was depressed during the last third of the century. It would have been difficult for an English economist of the period to talk of potential abundance when the industrial growth of his country appeared to have levelled off leaving a great deal of unrequited social misery.

[xv]

INTRODUCTION

The impressive transformation of the American economy did not automatically justify the belief that an age of abundance was possible. While some American social scientists were beginning to write about the implications of abundance, other men were worrying about America following the apparent course of European civilization from splendor to decay. Many Americans feared that the closing of the frontier as free land was exhausted and the thoughtless pillaging of natural resources would precipitate the decline of the young nation. Sophisticated men could not ignore the urgings of those who wanted to conserve natural resources and shut off the flood of immigrants in order to preserve the economic gains of the past. The rapid American transition from scarcity to abundance thus cut two ways. It justified optimism, but it also suggested that Americans must restrain the desires stimulated by their abundance or risk a new age of scarcity.

Many Americans, however, shared a group of internalized restraints which were later labelled the Protestant Ethic or, more precisely, worldly asceticism. Three attitudes are relevant to an understanding of Patten's conviction that abundance, properly controlled, would not be destroyed: the doctrine of the calling, the severe strictures against temptations of the flesh, and an intense commitment to the affairs of the world. Patten and such supporters as Walter E. Weyl and the sociologist Lester F. Ward, were, in general, confident that most of their countrymen could maintain appropriate restraint and that non-Protestant immigrants could be taught appropriate attitudes.

But it was difficult to retain confidence in theologically motivated restraints in an increasingly secular age. As biological and economic factors replaced God as the accepted cause of changes in the human condition, Patten began to suspect that the restraints of worldly asceticism were a result of the age-old struggle of men against nature for subsistence. Remove the need to struggle and the abundance created and maintained by hard work and dedicated abstinence might be destroyed. If scarcity reinforced restraint, supported traditional morality, it might be more valuable to the human race than the fruits of abundance.

Patten found a way out of this dilemma in another assumption he shared with many men of his generation: the belief that science could provide solutions to social problems. Specifically, science could develop and justify the restraints which would protect abundance from the evils of men's greed and the urges of the flesh. Drink, for example, which, in Protestant ethics, was held to make men sinful or less perfect, was forcefully condemned by the science of nutrition. Alcohol was unhealthy; it interfered with a man's consumption of a balanced diet, vitamins, and other necessities. Moreover, indulgence in drink could prevent a man from supplying his family with what we now call their minimum daily requirements.

Sex is another example. Before the development of modern biology and technology related to it, a man abstained from sleeping with his wife as a sign of his superiority over the flesh or his desire to limit the number of children he must provide for. Many women were what we now call frigid because nice women did not take pleasure in *that* sort of thing. Men with Patten's moral and ethical commitments could logically fear that abundance, by ending the struggle for subsistence, might produce a national orgy. Why avoid sexual pleasure if society can produce enough goods and services to sustain a larger population? Science provided clues to new restraints. The doctrines of eugenics —controlled heredity—convinced many people that they should mate after a careful assessment of the characteristics they would bestow on their progeny, not out of such unscientific feelings as affection or lust. Research and invention developed devices which would enable people to have sex without children: contraception enabled men to have the benefits of abundance and restraint at the same time.

Throughout his working life, Patten sought to justify his conviction that men could create and sustain an age of abundance by developing appropriate restraints. He alternated among arguments rooted in history, eco-

INTRODUCTION

nomics, science, and theology, never accepting any one set of justifications for more than a few years. In the first decade of the twentieth century, when *The New Basis of Civilization* was written, he was more concerned with the results of various techniques to create and maintain abundance than with finding authority for his convictions. This pragmatic period, however, came to an end during the First World War, which convinced Patten that it was necessary to probe more deeply into the causes of human behavior and social arrangements. In the last years of his life, he explored scientific materialism for clues to both the creation of abundance and the development of restraints. At the end of his life, however, he reasserted his earlier interest in theologically inspired restraints in uneasy ambivalence with his arguments for sanctions justified by science.

Patten never succeeded in synthesizing his ideas. Although he made several attempts to pull together the diverse strands in his thinking, they all ended in frustration. His ideas were presented in many forms; imbedded in carefully argued monographs about disputed questions of economics or sociology; in articles, or long digressions in works on economics, about the relationship between social science and such related areas of inquiry as ethics, education, social reform, and aesthetics; in confusingly written books attempting to relate the concepts of abundance and restraint to history, psychology, biology or the practices of economic and social life; and in popular articles dealing with contemporary public issues.

III

Patten's efforts to relate the concept of abundance to the economic and scientific thought of his time are exemplified in three books written in the twenty years before the publication of *The New Basis: The Premises of Political Economy* (1887), *The Theory of Dynamic Economics* (1892), and *The Theory of Social Forces* (1896).

The Premises of Political Economy, Patten's first full-length book, was the hesitant statement of a cautious and conscientious scholar who had begun to perceive the revolutionary consequences of rejecting the assumption of inevitable scarcity on which more than a century of economic thought had been built. Although his German training reinforced his desire to work out a new frame of reference, his study of English economists held him back. Patten claimed that his book was a "comment on certain positions of Mill similar to the comments of Mill on Adam Smith." In the course of commenting, Patten denied the doctrine of the niggardliness of nature which lay at the heart of classical economics, questioned the universal validity of Ricardo's Law of Rent, and denied the consistency of Darwin's theory of evolution with the seeming inexorability of Malthus' Law of Population. Combining the economic history and agricultural economics he had learned in Germany with his boyhood experiences in Illinois, he described ways in which the pressure of population against food supply could be reduced by increasing the variety of what was produced and reeducating consumers to desire goods which were in greater supply.[3]

In *The Premises*, the body of ideas known as Social Darwinism was in an uneasy relationship with Patten's knowledge of the effects of German social reform. Although Patten looked forward to an age of abundance, he worried that a "high civilization" had been developed "only in countries where the obstacles were so great that only the more intelligent could survive." Every improvement in techniques of production and habits of consumption removed obstacles which had prevented the weak from surviving.[4]

Unlike such conservative Social Darwinians as William Graham Sumner, however, Patten argued that men could use their intelligence to "improve on" what had been "given them by nature." The lower classes would "remain poor and ignorant" if they were not encouraged to "increase their intelligence" by state-supported education, enforcement of contract laws in favor of workers, limitation of consumer credit to prevent "slavery," and

[3]Simon N. Patten, *The Premises of Political Economy* (Philadelphia, 1885). The quotation is from a letter from Simon N. Patten to Richard T. Ely, February 20, 1900, Ely Papers, Box 8 (State Historical Society of Wisconsin).

[4]*The Premises*, pp. 216–217.

INTRODUCTION

restraint of the "speculative spirit" of capitalists in the interests of "public welfare." Progress, Patten believed, was hindered mainly by ignorance and prejudice, which could be removed by a higher standard of living, education, and increased opportunity.[5]

In *The Premises*, Patten's ideas moved toward encompassing the environments and value systems of Illinois and Germany, his experiences with both scarcity and potential abundance, and the classical and historical approaches to economics. Although he never succeeded in producing a coherent synthesis of these theories, he came closest to major rank as a social and economic thinker in two books written in the 1890's.

The central thesis of *The Theory of Dynamic Economics* (1892) was Patten's conviction that American society had become an "organic unity with a social mechanism that breaks up the slavish dependence of man on nature." The social mechanism responsible for the "dynamic economy" was a combination of productive techniques that enabled men to produce a surplus of goods and services with new attitudes developed as men adjusted to the era of abundance. Men's feelings and desires, translated into social arrangements and patterns of consumption, would determine the extent to which the surplus would grow or diminish. Patterns of consumption adjusted to what an environment could produce in greatest abundance, and social processes which

[5]*Ibid.*, pp. 221, 234, 236–237, 241.

enabled every citizen to contribute to and participate in abundance would prevent a return to scarcity. For instance, since full utilization of the goods and services produced by a society depended upon men having time to consume, more efficient methods of production, shorter working hours, and more equitable distribution of wealth were all necessary to maintain and increase national prosperity.[6]

After a lengthy economic analysis, involving modifications of conventional "static" notions of cost and value, Patten concluded that the surplus was the part of the "total utility" a society derived from its "economic environment" that remained to producers and consumers after costs and rent were paid. In a society like the United States, where wealth was distributed unequally, the "less fortunate classes" received "little of this surplus of utilities." The lower classes had only enough income to purchase "absolute utilities," goods necessary for survival. They lacked sufficient income to obtain goods which improved the quality of life.[7]

The complexity of the economic system, however, meant that more than redistribution of wealth was necessary to insure an improved standard of living for every citizen. The keys to improving the standard were abundance, restraint, and education. Improved

[6]Simon N. Patten, *The Theory of Dynamic Economics* (Philadelphia 1892), reprinted in Simon N. Patten, *Essays in Economics* (New York, 1924), pp. 43, 53, 55–57.
[7]*Ibid.*, pp. 81, 90.

techniques of production would increase the number and variety of goods available to consumers. Education would equip people to benefit from new goods and new combinations of goods and services. Experience with the fruits of abundance and moral education would force people to restrain "primitive appetites and passions" which would dissipate the surplus. Although higher wages "must precede" a rise in the standard of life of the working class, increased wages would have little effect if education in the use of new consumer goods did not occur simultaneously. New habits of consumption would erect a "subjective barrier to a fall in wages," since men would not tolerate renewed misery in an economy which produced an ever-increasing surplus.[8]

Poverty, in an economy of abundance, was a result of the selfishness of the prosperous classes, not of the niggardliness of nature. It was sustained by the "subjective conditions of producers," which could be modified by education and social reform. Patten wanted a concept of the "welfare of society" to replace the outmoded focus on the "welfare of individuals." In this way, feelings would be "generated" to "check the selfish actions of individuals." An abundance economy created new wants which could be "gratified only by concerted action of society."[9]

The American economic system had created the pos-

[8]*Ibid.*, pp. 113, 116.
[9]*Ibid.*, pp. 121, 123.

sibility of an economy of abundance. Patten sought ways to make the new economy a reality. He retained considerable respect for the techniques of capitalism. Despite his recommendations for the use of the surplus by the state, for example, he hoped that private investment capital would not be taxed out of existence. Men would often have to choose between "enjoying the surplus collectively and using it to keep society progressive." It was often necessary to "give up" part of the surplus to create prosperity; to admit that unequal distribution often stimulated economic growth more than the division of the product into equal shares.[10]

Despite his interest in increasing the working class's share of the national wealth, Patten attacked class politics as an inefficient means of achieving social progress. Class antagonism would disappear when society provided equality of education and opportunity. As the implications of the emerging economy of abundance were perceived, men would be more willing to allow the state to "retain their surplus for educational purposes." The state would use its share of the surplus to broaden the "scheme of education" in order to encourage the "productive qualities and feelings in men." Ultimately, each class would operate in terms of the same "psychical" premises, and the "feelings developed by the opposition of class interest" would disappear.[11]

[10] *Ibid.*, pp. 101–125.
[11] *Ibid.*, p. 127.

INTRODUCTION

Three years later, Patten tried to synthesize the economic, psychological, and reformist strands of his thought in *The Theory of Social Forces*. Social philosophy, he argued, must take account of a new relationship between men and their environment: "Human societies have at length emerged from the condition where the avoidance of pain is the requisite for survival. Man is now placed in a pleasure world and his needs demand a pleasure and not a pain economy." The social philosophy Patten erected on this premise was based on a restatement of ideas he had developed over the past decade. Evolution, the process of adjustment to new environments, was motivated by "competitive stress." This stress was the result of a reciprocal relationship between human intelligence and environments which constantly posed new challenges. Environmental change was dependent upon economic conditions.[12]

Neither economics nor theories of social evolution, however, revealed the "mental mechanism" which enabled men and external conditions to interact and produce changes in the "subjective environment." Patten sought the "mental mechanism" in the psychological doctrines developed in Germany, England, and the United States in the preceding two decades. The basis of Patten's psychology was a sharp distinction between sensory and motor ideas, which he related to

[12]Simon N. Patten, *The Theory of Social Forces* (Philadelphia, 1896), pp. 5, 7–9, 48.

[xxvi]

the concept of surplus pleasures. Sensory ideas, familiar from Lockean psychology, were impulses carried to the brain from the senses. Motor ideas, the impulses carried by the autonomic nervous system to the organs of the human body, caused "adjustment" between organisms and their environment. Patten criticized associationist psychology for conceiving of concepts as joined in "groups." These waves received their initial stimulus from the external environment. An environment which provided a surplus of pleasures stimulated the development of motor ideas. A surplus of pains, on the other hand, stimulated sensory ideas.[13]

Since motor impulses were stimulated by a surplus of pleasure in the environment, and the American economy was producing a growing surplus, it followed that motor impulses deserved more attention from social scientists. The problems of progress could be solved by stimulating particular motor responses. Simpler problems, the methods of increasing production or the proper patterns of consumption, for example, had already been solved or were approaching solution. Men had, however, learned to draw a surplus of pleasure from their environment without modifying their motor behavior: the beliefs, ideals, and passions which molded "social forces" had not changed to fit new economic conditions. Abundance made traditional values obsolete. Patten wanted to provide new values, to outline the changes in habits

[13]*Ibid.*, pp. 26, 40, 31, 37, 47.

and social patterns demanded by a unique economic situation; to harmonize economic reality and social attitudes.[14]

It would be necessary to create a society in which "man's mastery over nature" was complete while, at the same time, lethargy, vice, and overconsumption were restrained. Patten's vision of a future of restrained abundance implied a world governed by the absence of fear, not by the absence of pain. In a pain economy, men were forced to create institutions based on the "fear of enemies and pain." In the emerging pleasure economy, on the other hand, the "evils" were "subjective"—caused by "defective relations" between men or between man and nature. Internal evils, problems of "adjustment," had replaced the external threats of the age of scarcity. If the pleasure economy abolished restraints by eliminating all pain, the result would be greater misery than men had know in the age of scarcity.[15] Patten developed a model of a society which might survive and prosper. The "Social Commonwealth" demonstrated Patten's belief in the possibility of abundance tempered by restraint. Decisions would be made by "social impulse" rather than by "conscious calculation." These decisions would stimulate new ideals which would create new institutions. The first new ideals would be economic: methods of producing

[14]*Ibid.*, pp. 51–53.
[15]*Ibid.*, pp. 75, 77, 122.

and distributing wealth. The second set of ideals would be "aesthetic" and would transform the consumption of wealth by stimulating changes leading to its "best utilization." Third, new moral ideals would limit the activities of individuals to those fields where "future welfare" was "prominent." Finally, religious ideals would illuminate the "defects and limitations of our planetary existence" and suggest another world where the "possibilities of perfect existence" could be realized. The Social Commonwealth would not be the "highest or even a final social state." It would not be able to "satisfy all the aspirations of men." Patten was building a model, not planning a utopia.[16]

Patten's ideals were not unique. Throughout his life he clung to the liberal dream, the ethics of the New Testament as reshaped by the productive capacities of the Industrial Revolution. He would have agreed with John Maynard Keynes's hope that "perhaps a day might come when there would be enough to go round. . . . In that day overwork, overcrowding, and underfeeding would come to an end, and men, secure of the comforts and necessities of the body, could proceed to the nobler exercise of their faculties."[17] Unlike most of his contemporaries, however, Patten believed that the materials and tools were at hand with which to implement

[16]*Ibid.*, pp. 81, 84–85, 92–94.
[17]John Maynard Keynes, *The Economic Consequences of the Peace* (London, 1919), p. 21.

the liberal dream and that some social planning was necessary to prevent needless suffering in the evolutionary process. Yet Patten was not sure how much suffering was needless or how much planning would do more harm than good. He refused to disregard the nagging fear that unrestrained abundance might turn potential paradise into hell.

Patten tried, almost desperately, to mold his contradictory feelings and ideas into a coherent system in the second half of *The Theory of Social Forces*. He tried, for instance, to combine recognition of the need for new institutions with fear of the results of their operation. "In order to survive in the Social Commonwealth," each person must join a "group of producers." Individuals who insisted on "working with their hands or by themselves" would eventually "be forced into such a condition of want that disease and vice would carry them off." These ideas were, however, qualified by an inconsistent affection for the social forms of an age of scarcity: "In many respects the institutions of the Social Commonwealth would operate in a manner more like those of the Middle Ages that those of the present century." Moreover, the new institutions would have to be small and should not grow too quickly.[18]

Patten was ambivalent about the relationship between democratic ideals and the development of the Social Commonwealth. He was pleased that the blend-

[18]Patten, *Social Forces*, pp. 86, 98–99.

ing of local environments into one general environment had "given increased vigor to the democratic ideal," and looked forward to reducing "immobility and subordination among individuals." Yet he feared that democracy might "hinder further differentiation and tend to keep in society all the classes it now contains." The maintenance of equality at a time when the values of abundance were struggling to displace the values of scarcity prevented the development of men with appropriate "civic instincts."[19]

Nevertheless, Patten concluded *The Theory of Social Forces* by emphasizing social solidarity and improved consumption rather than increasing differentiation among men. It was better, for example, to provide "general measures of relief" against distress and inadequate adjustment to the new basis of civilization than to encourage citizens to rely on "their own efforts." He reaffirmed his thesis that progress was the result of the increasingly sophisticated calculation of subjective utility. Yet he had posed several disturbing questions. Patten's dilemmas were postponed rather than resolved.[20]

IV

The New Basis of Civilization, written as a series of lectures a decade after *The Theory of Social Forces*, re-

[19]*Ibid.*, pp. 16, 127, 130, 138–140, 142.
[20]*Ibid.*, pp. 92–93, 148, 151.

flected Patten's decision to put his dilemmas aside and relate his convictions and theories to the practical problem of eradicating the causes and effects of poverty in America. From 1905 to 1918, his efforts to promote active adaptation to the emerging economy of abundance compensated for his failure to construct a coherent social theory.

The development of Patten's conviction that poverty could be abolished and the good life for all achieved if men accepted values and restraints appropriate to abundance coincided with the growth of professional philanthropy in America. The new and uncertain profession of social work experienced a remarkable growth in the 1890's. Charity Organization Societies, introduced from England in the 1880's to systematize the distribution of private relief funds, gained control of philanthropic activities in most large cities. Settlement Houses, established in the 1890's and led by such passionate and articulate persons as Jane Addams and Lillian Wald, were growing in size, number, and prestige. Professional training for social workers began at the turn of the century.

The development of professional social work was both a cause and a result of a change in attitudes toward poverty in Europe and the United States in the decades around the turn of the century. As the productive power of the West increased, scholars and reformers in Germany, England, and the United States subjected the traditional theory of poverty to empirical investigation. They discovered that drunkenness, sloth, and mendacity, the vices of the "undeserving" poor, were usually the results rather than the causes of poverty. A few men, the English scholars Charles Booth, John A. Hobson, and Seebohm Rowntree, for instance, suggested that the existence of poverty placed limits on economic growth. When Patten applied his insight into the emergence of an age of abundance to the problems of economic suffering, a new theory of poverty, which had nothing to do with morality, was beginning to emerge. The new theory, axiomatic to many men in the mid-twentieth century, was untenable to men who assumed that scarcity was the normal condition of life. According to the new theory, poverty is an economic phenomenon that can and must be abolished. Moreover, the state is the only social institution with sufficient resources to deal with the complex economic and social forces that create poverty.

Patten tried to interest his students in social work from the early 1890's. He arranged for courses on the problems of understanding and dealing with poverty to be given at the University of Pennsylvania, and obtained jobs in social service agencies for interested students. In 1896, Edward T. Devine, who received a doctorate under Patten, became General Secretary of the New York Charity Organization Society. For the next quarter-century, Devine was the nation's leading philanthropic executive—administrative head of several organizations, founder of the New York School of Social Work, editor of *Charities* magazine, and the first Professor of Social Legislation at Columbia. In 1938, Devine recalled that in the first two decades of the century he had had regular conferences with Patten about policies and programs. Patten had "far more to do with developments in social work" for which Devine had the "main credit" than anyone had ever realized.[21]

In 1905, Devine and another former student of Patten's, Samuel M. Lindsay, Professor of Social Welfare at Columbia, established the annual Kennedy Lectureship at the New York School of Social Work. For the first lecturer they chose Patten, mainly to publicize his ideas to the profession but also to lift him out of the depression into which he had fallen after his failure to produce a coherent synthesis of his ideas. The text, heavily edited by Patten's wife and published as *The New Basis of Civilization* in 1907, was written in a flowing evangelical style, quite different from the tortured, often turgid prose of his other work. *The New Basis* became Patten's most popular and influential book; it went through eight editions in the next sixteen years.

Patten stated his concept of cultural lag more succinctly than ever before: "The economic revolution is

[21]Edward T. Devine, *When Social Work Was Young* (New York, 1938), p. 20.

here," but the "intellectual revolution that will rouse men to its stupendous meaning has not done its work." Despite a "surplus stored by cooperative effort," Americans retained "ancient social emotions" which prevented them from adapting to abundance. In the contemporary United States, there was a contrast between the "surfeited and the exploited," between those who consumed too much and those who had too little. This contrast could only be removed by social action to restrain the surfeited and provide opportunities for the exploited.[22]

In this polemic form, Patten's theory of cultural lag was quite different from the lag theory made famous by William F. Ogburn of the University of Chicago two decades later. The concept of a lag between environmental change and men's perception of its implications was not original with either Patten or Ogburn. It was an obvious deduction from the theoretical framework of the branch of sociology which emphasized imitation, invention, attitudes, and roles. Academic sociologists considered two varieties of lag: cultural, the maladjustment of social organization to changes in technology; and biological, the lack of adjustment between human nature and culture. The doctrine of cultural lag assumed the possibility of evolutionary change toward a

[22]The page citations of the quotations from *The New Basis of Civilization* that appear in this paragraph, and those of others that follow hereafter, will not ordinarily be given.

society with fewer tensions and conflicts. Biological lag, on the other hand, was a conservative doctrine. Men like the French scholar, Gustav LeBon, and the Americans, Franklin H. Giddings and Ogburn, often treated culture as a thin veneer over a fundamental human savagery which showed few signs of change. Although Patten had explored the possibility of biological lag in his earlier work, he disregarded it on *The New Basis*. As a moralist of abundance, anxious to get his message to a large audience, he put aside annoying possibilities.

The lag between the surfeited and the exploited raised a special problem for America because the poor were becoming less visible to their affluent countrymen. Civilization increasingly spared men the "sight of anguish." The imaginations of affluent men must be "sharpened to see in the checkbook an agent as spiritual and poetic as the grime and bloodstain of ministering hands." Patten emphasized the importance of money— private and public—in raising the standard of life of the poor. In an age of abundance, men must recognize the ideological value of cash. Money, properly spent, would release "pent forces" far better than the moral platitudes of "Service Altruism"—the traditional technique of philanthropic workers. Patten preferred "Economic Altruism"—the willingness to "bestow without conditions and to be taxed for public and far-reaching ends"—to the well-intentioned "paternal kindness that opens picture galleries to the public."

Money in the hands of social workers could be used to abolish poverty. Like Lenin, who called for trained revolutionary cadres to implement Marx's theory of inevitable revolution, Patten wanted social workers to implement the age of abundance. But he was a shrewd and cautious man. Although he had little faith in alms-giving, he knew that social workers, the cadres of progress, needed the sympathy and financial support of the middle and upper classes. Accordingly, he refrained from advocating comprehensive social and economic planning to raise the standard of living.

Instead of making a frontal attack on middle class philanthropists, Patten obliquely criticized affluent Americans for ignoring the importance of group action as a tool for eradicating poverty. If philanthropists embraced Patten's belief in the importance of group life, they could stimulate new ideals of human behavior appropriate to an economy of abundance. America had "ample resources" to "abolish poverty by saving men instead of spending them." Men who praised the "disciplinary values of hardship" and "rewarded those who acquired them" had not transcended the age of scarcity. Philanthropists should channel money to social workers who would teach the lower classes how variety in consumption could relieve the "inevitable monotony of work in the machine age" and stimulate agitation for higher wages and shorter working hours. In the history of American attacks on poverty, Patten, as a theoretician, stands halfway between Andrew Carnegie and Saul Alinsky.

Social workers could also inculcate restraints to protect the age of abundance from gluttony and vice. They might, for example, encourage men to take pleasure in the arts rather than in eating, drinking, and sexual indulgence. Patten's view of aesthetics was similar to that of Jane Addams and other leading social workers. Unlike Miss Addams' views, however, Patten's were part of a complex intellectual structure: the theory of consumption he had been developing for twenty years. Like the settlement workers, Patten preferred active participation in the arts to passive appreciation of prescribed values. Patten went beyond most of his contemporaries, however, when he defined such group activities as national holiday celebrations, camp meetings, and circuses as "culture." Social workers must take advantage of existing institutions—fraternal, political, economic, and cultural—which, by creating "bonds of control," enabled men to develop restraints against the evils of abundance.

Patten's tone was pragmatic, but he still could not avoid the dilemmas that had plagued him during the previous fifteeen years. He warned that poverty would be "scarcely mitigated by prosperity," that it might be "many thousand" years before men were completely adjusted to abundance, and that, lacking convincing authority for his views, he was unsure of the long-range effects of his proposals. Moreover, he was ambivalent about the goals of social work. He believed social workers must "go beyond the test of personality and family . . . and set up the standard of each locality as the norm by which the defects . . . of the poor are to be measured." On the next page, however, Patten offered to measure the success of social workers by the "number of independent, self-supporting families" they created.

Pragmatism won out over despair. Social workers should be concerned with means, not ends. The ends of progress could not be defined. They would be attained, paradoxically, only when men lost "sight of them in the struggle for material improvements." It would be sufficient for social workers to concentrate on "moving people from the margin instead of aiding them at the margin"—to realize that the preconditions for the disappearance of poverty were the "extension of opportunity, the growth of efficiency, the spread of knowledge, and the increase of health."

Patten's program for social work contained many of the same reforms advocated by the social justice movement in America and the "New Liberalism" in England. Like such American contemporaries as Jane Addams,

INTRODUCTION

Florence Kelley, Robert LaFollette, and Louis D. Brandeis, Patten wanted public guarantees of better standards of income, working conditions, health and housing. Unlike Patten, however, these reformers emphasized the removal of abuses rather than the formulation of a positive program to improve the future. The English reformers, Sidney and Beatrice Webb, William Beveridge, and David Lloyd George, however, were not content with removal of existing abuses. The years between 1905 and 1912, when *The New Basis of Civilization* was most influential in America, were years of ferment in English reform. The Webbs's Minority Report on the Poor Law and agitation for a "national minimum," Beveridge's program for unemployment compensation, and Lloyd George's health insurance legislation anticipated analogous American reforms by more than a generation. Patten's persuasive argument that social workers should "fix the responsibility of the state in caring for the health and welfare of its citizens" placed him in the vanguard of later American agitation for social legislation.

Although Patten's central theme, that the goal of social action is adaptation to the economy of abundance, is part of the ideology of many contemporary social workers, *The New Basis* sparked a controversy in the young profession when it appeared. Patten's leading supporters were Devine, Frances Perkins, then with the Consumers' League, and Lillian Wald, director of the

Henry Street Settlement in New York. His most powerful opponent was Mary Richmond, ideologist of social work as the response of dedicated individuals to the problems of impoverished individuals and families and director of the Philadelphia Charity Organization Society. Miss Richmond, a pioneer in developing the techniques of casework, was deeply disturbed by Patten's preference for group over individual action. She attacked his proposal that social workers agitate for the elimination of the causes of poverty. There was no relation between "money power" and "effective charity." No legislation could substitute for the "neighborly service of the Samaritan." The debate between Patten's and Miss Richmond's supporters brought into focus the major issues of dispute and uncertainty in the field of social welfare: the relative value of professional and voluntary workers, the respective merits of philanthropic and political action, the influence of social work on social change, and the attitudes of social workers toward such public issues as the cost of living, economic crises, social insurance, immigration restriction, and prohibition.[23]

Miss Richmond reflected deeply held convictions and spoke for powerful forces within professional social work when she challenged Patten's ideas. Patten emphasized

[23]Mary R. Richmond, *The Good Neighbor* (Philadelphia, 1907), p. 17. For the history of social work in this period, see Clarke E. Chambers, *Seedtime of Reform* (Minneapolis, 1963) and Roy Lubove, *The Professional Altruist* (Cambridge, 1965).

the need for group action to provide economic opportunity, education, and social justice to the large number of people who were poor because they were powerless, uninformed, or victims of prejudice. At the same time, many leading social workers, for a variety of reasons, were attempting to commit the profession to casework or groupwork aimed at removing psychological and educational barriers to adjustment in American society. Where Patten advocated changing the environment and reforming laws and institutions, those who were gaining control of the institutions and resources of social work increasingly preferred to accept existing economic and social arrangements or to expect only gradual environmental change. Moreover, at a time when social work depended on philanthropy bestowed from altruistic motives, and many social workers took spiritual comfort from the acts of giving with which they and their sponsors improved the world, Patten raised questions about the utility of love, or even stewardship, to increase the wealth and develop the productive skills of poor people, and was prepared to encourage social conflict in order to achieve a better society.

Although *The New Basis* was reissued eight times between 1907 and 1915, in the 1950's and 1960's Patten's ideas had to be reintroduced into professional social work in other forms and by men who had never heard of Simon Patten. The style of thinking about social problems expressed by Patten in 1905 did not become a

INTRODUCTION

viable style for men and women who earn their livings by helping the poor until it became painfully obvious that casework and groupwork had not notably reduced the number of poor people in America; until Negroes, the largest identifiable group among the American poor, had begun to force legal and institutional change by organization, conflict, and coalition without the aid of many professional social workers; and until the notion that it is possible to provide a decent standard of living for all without massive redistribution of wealth—the concept of abundance—had become part of the conventional wisdom.

It would be wrong, however, to credit Patten with being a premature exponent of the kinds of programs mounted by the Civil Rights Movement or the Office of Economic Opportunity. Patten realized in 1920 that *The New Basis* had passed its point of influence. He lashed out at social workers for embracing casework, "a vain struggle against impossibilities" when more than half the American people needed to be educated, medically cared for, and organized to enjoy the potential benefits of an age of abundance. Moreover, he knew that the helping professions had rejected his notion that the final solution for poverty lay in "institutional measures"—legal and structural changes—to extend the standards of middle class life to all Americans.[24]

[24]Simon N. Patten, "Backsliding on Social Work," *Survey*, 44 (June 5, 1920), 338–343.

INTRODUCTION

But Patten was a theoretician who never sought actively enough for programs which would put his theories into practice. He was a strategist who suffered from not caring about or understanding tactics. For *The New Basis* to have sparked an underground movement, within or outside the profession of social work, Patten or someone close to him would have had to train a cadre of technicians and mount programs based on Patten's strategies. Rexford Tugwell, in a different profession, and Edward Devine and Frances Perkins within social work, shared Patten's assumption and notions about means and ends. They did not, however, seek to create a movement.

For a generation, the concept of abundance was synonymous with Simon Patten. He raised issues which still disturb those who speculate about ways to improve the quality of American life. During the past fifteen years, many men have accepted the possibility of a transformation from scarcity to abundance as the basis of economic and social life. The most frequently debated issues have been whether social theorists can talk of an affluent society as an established fact or a potential condition, and the implications for social policy of the existence or the approach of abundance. It is one thing to agree that social policy shall be concerned with *optima* rather than *minima;* quite another to define the content of the good life. It is easier to

INTRODUCTION

decide that men must restrain certain feelings and desires than to find effective ways to inculcate these restraints. There is considerable confusion about definitions, means, and ends in contemporary thought and action based on the assumption of abundance. Whether the assumption first stated systematically by Simon Patten is to be the basis of a profound change in the human condition, or merely another in the long list of curiously naive American opinions, still remains to be seen.

Daniel M. Fox
April, 1968

A NOTE ON THE TEXT

The New Basis of Civilization has been reproduced photographically from a copy of the original 1907 edition which bore the imprint of The Macmillan Company, New York, and Macmillan & Co., Ltd., London.

AMERICAN SOCIAL PROGRESS SERIES

THE NEW
BASIS OF CIVILIZATION

BY

SIMON N. PATTEN, Ph.D., LL.D.

PROFESSOR OF POLITICAL ECONOMY, WHARTON SCHOOL OF
FINANCE AND COMMERCE, UNIVERSITY OF
PENNSYLVANIA

THE KENNEDY LECTURES FOR 1905, IN THE SCHOOL OF
PHILANTHROPY, CONDUCTED BY THE CHARITY
ORGANIZATION SOCIETY OF THE CITY
OF NEW YORK

New York
THE MACMILLAN COMPANY
LONDON: MACMILLAN & CO., Ltd.
1907

PREFACE BY THE EDITOR

THE American Social Progress Series is designed to furnish the increasing number of students of our concrete American social life, especially in its manifestation in social problems that have arisen in the larger cities of the United States, a series of brief and clearly written handbooks, stating the newer social thought based upon the accumulated material of recent scientific investigations. Some of the volumes, for which plans are in progress, will be chiefly descriptive, and embody the results of such field investigation of the facts relating to special problems as we have recorded for English conditions in the works of Mr. Charles Booth, Mr. Rowntree, and others. Brevity of statement and conciseness of treatment will be maintained so that these handbooks may be serviceable for collateral reading and class discussion in the various groups of persons, who, in our colleges and educational institutions as well as in clubs and literary societies, are giving attention and study to the social problems of our own time.

PREFACE

The volume by Professor Patten makes an admirable introduction to such a series. It interprets in a specially suggestive and stimulating way the meaning and significance of recent social changes with which the practical social worker is so actively engaged and to which he is so close in point of time and contact that he may well fail to secure for himself the stimulus of the larger outlook upon the events in which he is a participant.

Professor Patten desires to acknowledge, with gratitude, his obligations to his wife, Charlotte Kimball Patten, for her assistance in the statement of the doctrines contained in this book and in its preparation for publication.

SAMUEL McCUNE LINDSAY.

NEW YORK CITY,
March 19, 1907.

CONTENTS

CHAPTER I

THE BASIS IN RESOURCES

CHAPTER I

THE BASIS IN RESOURCES

ONE summer day I took my note-book to a wooded hillside whence I could overlook a rich and beautiful valley. The well-tended farms, the strong stone houses, the busy men and animals moving peacefully over roads and fields, would inspire me, I was sure, with the opening theme of this book. As I seated myself under a chestnut tree a fellow-guest at the hotel came by, and glancing at my memoranda asked if I, like himself, was writing a lecture. He too had come to the woods, he said, to meditate and to be inspired by nature. But his thesis, enthusiastically unfolded, was the opposite to mine. It was a part of his faith as a Second Adventist that the world is becoming more unhappy and more wicked; and it is now so evil that the end of it approaches. On the face of the earth are wars and in the air rumors of war. Disease, famine, and disaster surround us; vice reigns, moral decay spreads, and only the annihilation of mankind can satisfy divine justice and purify the way for the practice of the long-deferred divine plan. To find inspiration for this text

[3]

my companion had also come to look upon the
teeming farm lands owned by clean and well-housed
folk.   Where I marked the progress of humanity and
thrilled with the hope that poverty will soon be ban-
ished from the world as it has been from this happy
valley, he saw a threatening scene of worldliness where
prosperity lulled spiritual alarms to a dangerous moral
peace.   The general argument that degeneration follows a prolonged period of material success is familiar
to the reader, and I need not give the outline colored
by the social and religious philosophy of his sect.
Yet in spite of the fundamental differences in our
training it seemed strange to me that two men looking at the same picture could agree wholly upon the
truths it painted and forthwith interpret them as dif-
ferently as we did.   Looking down into this plentiful
valley, one fortified his belief that divine wrath must
be invoked upon a region carnal and depraved; while
the other joyfully exclaimed, "Here is the basis of a
new civilization; here is evidence that economic forces
can sweep away poverty, banish misery, and by giving
men work bring forth right and enduring character
within the race."

The electicism of the Adventist's views reminded me
of a social reformer with whom I had talked not long
before.   I had recalled to this cultured University

man — what he of course knew perfectly well — the series upon series of improvements in the conditions of workingmen's lives which are steadily following economic changes now going on; I reminded him of numerous pleasure-yielding motives to work which have been given to the poor; and I pointed out the familiar truth that their consumption of goods has been enormously increased, widely varied, and remarkably cheapened. He nodded his head affirmatively after these statements: then he quickly shook it in negation, saying, "I have lived in Berlin, Paris, London, New York, and Chicago, and in all of them the misery of the masses is as acute as it ever was." His selective vision settled at once upon large cities where his own life centred about the struggling poor. He waived my evidence as having little bearing on urban poverty, while he seemed to me to be incompletely measuring social progress by symptoms, effects, and local hindrances. Acquaintance with the condition of the poor remains for him a basis broad enough to define the forces beneath our civilization; I believe we approach truth only when we construct our theories from a study of continental resources and a precise knowledge of the effects of inventions and improvements in modes of life upon whole populations.

I mention these conversations because they typify a

kind now carried on between men with differing educations. Each disputant comes into the field with an experience gained in one of the many environments which our great world affords, and from its vantage ground, armed with its sympathies and interests, draws local deductions to which he gives a universal application. If men in the same place disagreed upon the main facts within it, or if men in different places refused to accept each other's evidence, then there would be no hope of blending, explaining, and reconstructing these particular experiences into a general and comprehensive viewpoint. But in reality there is surprisingly little difference of opinion concerning the facts within the environments that may be discussed. Few men deny that the working people of industrial centres are ill paid, that employment is uncertain, housing is bad, sickness frequent, and that the abnormally short working life ends in an old age of poverty and fear. There are few, on the other hand, who deny the evidence of growing prosperity. Prosperity is a fact: and so is poverty. Both are too evident to be contested.

The differences of opinion develop from the interpretation of facts. We cannot survey to-day's occurrences as isolated phenomena uninfluenced by yesterday's conditions from which they issued. Neither can we prophesy what will be the effects to-morrow of to-day's events by looking backward to see what followed similar circumstances in remote times. Nevertheless, when men do undertake to interpret to-day and to-morrow they turn their gaze to the past, search there for resembling situations, and having found one or more, use them as premises to the conclusion that what followed in the first case will also follow in the present instance. They confuse the law that like effects follow like causes into the loose axiom that history repeats itself. If two men differ radically about the lessons to be drawn from an historical epoch, they will differ as radically about the future consequences of a present situation at the very moment when they are in entire accord upon the actual data under their eyes. They may visit a country together and note a score of evidences of its prosperity; yet one will conclude that good times are temporary and must inevitably be followed by the accustomed misery and exploitation, while the other stoutly affirms that here is the beginning of a new epoch which is without historical precedent, and which may therefore endure indefinitely longer than the Greek or Roman city cited by his friend. If they walk the squalid streets of a factory town and mark the sodden suffering, one will exclaim that this is the predicted outcome of the exploitation of the workers under present methods of pro-

duction; the other replies that it is the lingering consequences of social injustice and nature's early violences
which modern science and industry are relieving, but
which they have not had time to eradicate. The issue
in neither case is drawn wholly from the local situation;
it is determined by the relative importance the men
attach to similar circumstances in bygone eras.

To arrive at a man's opinions one ought to know
what he has read and heard rather than what he has
seen. The glasses through which we scan the present
have been ground, polished, and focussed by the experience of the race in distant ages, and we behold most
distinctly the objects at a distance. It is difficult,
therefore, to interpret the present according to its own
significance, and more difficult still to understand the
past through our knowledge of the present. But a
careful reversal of the popular method of reasoning
would give a clearer view of contemporary life and a
corrected impression of the past. It would begin with a
scrutiny of to-day, retrace history, and predict the future
from a knowledge tested by joint studies of the two.
The other mode of thinking threads an involved path
starting in historical episodes, makes a detour around
the present, and leads to a goal in the future where its
followers expect to find new episodes like those they
began with. The one is an economic, the other an his-

torical interpretation. Are we nearer the truth when we hold that like economic antecedents produce like social effects or that like historical antecedents will produce like future results? Shall we search for our postulates among the economic and geographic conditions in which we live or shall we return to the history of our crudest ancestral type?

The choice is fundamentally important and divides social thinkers into opposing camps. Those who would predict to-morrow's economic states from a study of the economic states of Rome or Venice overlook the difference between a society struggling to meet a deficit and one so well situated that thought can be centred on the equitable distribution of a surplus. In the one case the civilization must develop its traditions to keep the deficit as small as possible and eventually to overcome it, and in the other to utilize the surplus for common good, not to undermine energy and productive ability or to create parasitic classes, but to distribute the surplus in ways that will promote general welfare and secure better preparation for the future. The one type of society may be called a pain or deficit economy, the other a pleasure or surplus economy. All civilizations before the nineteenth century, like the primitive societies of the Western world to-day and the backward despotisms of the East, were realms of

[9]

pain and deficit, in which the traditions and experiences of men were moulded out of the general menaces to life and happiness. When adjustment to nature was defective at many points and lacking altogether at others, forecasts of evil were proved true by the event, and men learned to expect calamity and disorder. If nations established themselves in rich localities where they might have built stable institutions upon natural resources, other nations warred upon them without let or hindrance, and the contests exhausted the land. In short, the story of the rise and fall of nations, repeated again and again, seems to justify the familiar conclusion that the decline of a society after an epoch of prosperity is a natural, incontrovertible law. But are these sad endings the fit sequels of man's ill-doing in a one-time perfect world, as certain moralists have affirmed, or are suffering and defeat the outcome of the purely physical conditions of existence? If the latter, improvements in the environment will construct a new basis for civilization by lessening deficit and destroying the old status between men and nature.

We must admit that such a process of amelioration in world affairs is going on. But the changes wrought by that process are so recent that the effects of old conditions have not disappeared. They persist in a revolutionized order of things which has not yet definitely reconstructed the traditions and orthodox modes of thought. Mental habits continue long after the economic conditions which fashioned them have disappeared, and popular beliefs reflect the passing age of nature's deficit, while the actions of men who hold those beliefs are chiefly governed by the new age of surplus in which they live. The economic revolution is here, but the intellectual revolution that will rouse men to its stupendous meaning has not done its work.

The static condition of men's minds is revealed by the contradictions of current thought, and by premises drawn from data that have ceased to be true. John Stuart Mill is still warmly upheld when he says that the science of economics rests upon the niggardliness of nature. Teachers lay down the Law of Diminishing Returns as emphatically as ever, and expound afresh the sweeping Malthusian doctrine of population. We still tremble at the growth of numbers, and advocate measures to restrict the movement of races from poorer to better surroundings. How many there are who fear a lower wage and greater poverty as the bitter fruit of the throngs of eager workers who press into our ports!

It was the social philosophy of deficit that brought forth the theory of exploitation, and its derivative the Iron Law of Wages, which working men and socialists uphold as ardently as the upper classes do the principles of Mill and Ricardo. In another form it becomes the Single Tax doctrine advanced by Henry George. His followers teach us that good lands and advantageous sites are scarce, and that multitudes are degraded by the pressure forcing them downward to poor locations.

In history this ancient outlook is described in terms of the decadence of places and the degeneration of peoples. In politics the masses are pronounced unworthy of trust, hero-worship is practised, imperialism and government by the few are advocated, and the continuance of military and police power is correspondingly assured.

Shift the viewpoint once more, and race hatreds are explained as the result of the necessary strife for possession of the limited riches of the earth. We define civilization so narrowly that we cast out people who live beyond the frost line. And then we limit it to those who eat wheat and meat. We postulate the excellences of men who dwell in mountainous regions and exclude the servile lowlander. We extol those of country birth to the disadvantage of the dwellers of towns, and ban Southern races because tradition makes them passionate. Reason, our philosophy tells us, is a quality of men who live in cold regions; emotion sways the people of warm countries. A similar contrast is made between the white and dark races, and the elect are further limited

[12]

by the assumed superiority of the Aryan stock. Popular government, we assert, can exist only among the Germans, or perhaps only among the Anglo-Americans. These varied doctrines logically construct a pervasive philosophy that limits the conditions of civilization and progress to a few localities, and marks as ineligible candidates persons of other races and places than our own; so that for the majority of men the future is dubious enough. But have nature's negations remained absolute and are subsistence wars still the principle of social evolution? Do resources diminish with use? Indications of a stupendous change have been accumulating for many years, but their profound significance has been slurred by writers whose eyes have been fixed upon the spectacular history of society. An agriculture that added to nature's endowment was feebly practised here and there while the Law of Diminishing Returns was being written; mother countries were becoming reluctant to denude their colonies of pelts, timber, ivories, and human beings; and England in India was learning to sow scientifically with one hand in order that she might longer reap with the other. But this faint stirring was unnoticed behind the body of facts with which thinkers were dealing. It is as if they were engaged in writing the epilogue of one drama while the curtain was rising upon the prologue of another presenting a new cast of characters. Much of the scenery to-day is that with which time has made us familiar, and the action seems to follow the ancient tragic model. There is the old motive of exploitation; the stronger men use the weaker, and having destroyed them in their machinery of production, discard them while they are still in their middle life; they capture children and torture the little prisoners of industry; and they prey on the women inside factory walls. Bands of men in great cities undergo disease, hunger, exposure, and contend savagely with shifting masses of immigrants who are a steady overtax upon the local labor market. The lives of the weakest in crowded towns seem still ordered by the Law of Diminishing Returns. But here the new players intervene and promise that millions of the weak shall be added to industrial civilization without the tragic climax of starvation, disease, and despair. Many of the obstacles that were insuperable a century ago are falling before the young genius of the mechanical age. Militarism, bad sanitation, inadequate protection from heat and cold, a high birth-rate offsetting a high death-rate — all these obstructions to the broadened consuming power of the poor have been reduced. Ground that lay barren because of ignorance and scarcity of capital and of tools is fertile now because there are tools and money for every feat of agriculture.

Immobile masses of men used to die of famine while a few hundred miles away crops rotted on the ground for lack of transportation. Famine no longer threatens a country where railroads carry freight. United States laboratories and food stations are evolving cereals and condensing nutriment in their tissues. Government experts are studying food for men and cattle on the Russian steppes and in half-forgotten oases of the Sahara. Mr. Luther Burbank hopes to overcome nature in the deserts of the West with the science-born thornless cactus; he doubles the size of fruits and brings new ones into being, in a few years outdistancing the pace of thousands of generations of his "master," — nature. The Secretary of Agriculture recently declared that serious crop failures will occur no more. Agriculture has become a science, our common foods grow in conquered habitats, the desert is sown, and waste land is made fertile. Unseasonable frosts, prolonged droughts and rains, torrid heat, insect pests, plant disease — all these familiar menaces he believes will soon cease to threaten the farmer. Never again will widespread famine, plagues, scarcity prices, or commercial panics be the result of defective husbandry. Stable, progressive farming controls the terror, disorder, and devastation of earlier times. A new agriculture means a new civilization. Physicians and sanitarians tell us that the

[15]

recent yellow fever epidemic was the last which shall find foothold in the United States. Their knowledge of its causes gives them power to subdue it. To recall the horror that has accompanied the plague since history began is to foresee what a change in social traditions and industrial development this revolution alone will make. The food, housing, and general hygiene of the workers at Panama, for instance, can be cared for so scientifically that the canal will be dug under conditions possible fifty years ago only north of the frost line.

Each gain upon nature adds to the quantity of goods to be consumed by society, and lessens the labor necessary to produce them. Improved conditions make better men, and better men improve conditions. Professor Shaler says men can double the food supply of the world by expansion of population and double that by engineering devices; if it be true, American possibilities exceed even his amazing estimate, for we occupy one of the most fertile regions of the globe. The fall in the rate of business, the eagerness to invest daringly, the alertness of capital to enter new business, the widespread security of investments, the "saving instinct" which has become a constant, half-automatic pressure toward the growth of funds, — these economic truths have been so minutely illustrated by special observers that it is scarcely necessary to assume a general doubt of

[16]

the nation's present ability to give work to hordes of men equipped with an average physique and some intelligence. Prince Kropotkin epitomizes the change when he writes: "For the first time in the history of civilization, mankind has reached a point where the means of satisfying its needs are in excess of the needs themselves. To impose, therefore, as has hitherto been done, the curse of misery and degradation upon vast divisions of mankind, in order to secure well-being for the few, is needed no more; well-being can be secured for all, without overwork for any. We are thus placed in a position entirely to remodel the very bases and contents of our civilization — provided the civilized nations find in their midst the constructive capacities and the powers of creation required for utilizing the conquests of the human intellect in the interest of all."

The well-being of which the Russian reformer thought doubtless differs greatly from that which men pronounced fair a few years ago. At the beginning of the factory system the standards of comfort for laborers were so low that prosperity was defined as nothing more than free and steady access to the two or three staple foods produced in the workers' localities. Cheapness signified control over the few good foods of each community rather than access to the supplies of a continent. Adam Smith, not dreaming of a transportation system

c　　　[17]

which would shortly organize the resources of a world, named the essentials of civilization "cheapness and plenty"; he probably meant by that the ability to buy bread and potatoes, or whatever the laborer's environment produced in largest quantities. At that time the food area was measured by a narrow belt through the North Temperate Zone, and estimated by the accessible amount of wheat. Now, although wheat in our markets grows close to the polar circle, it has not kept its ancient position as chief resource of the workingman, because the multiplication of other cheap edibles places options upon the laborer's table. The grocery window stacked with "breakfast foods," unimagined ten years ago, witnesses at the same time that the use of non-wheat products has increased the demand for cereals in astonishing multiples. Less monotonous, more palatable, and very easily prepared, these "ready to eat" goods are perhaps the cheapest, in proportion to nutrition and to labor-power saved, that have yet been found. They economize fuel, and they set free a fraction of the housewife's time — it is asserted that they were devised to simplify the servant problem in the houses of the well-to-do. If it is true that certain varieties selling at seven or eight cents are properly accused of lacking the ingredients included in the chemical formula on the box, and are nothing more than simple cereal flakes, they

[18]

"go further" than a loaf of bread and have two valuable qualities beside: they increase the demand for sugar and milk, and they vary the diet.

No manipulation of a corner can permanently raise the price of bread, for the "natural monopoly" was broken when wheat first came to market from the edge of the tropics and the polar latitudes. In Western America extensive cultivation of it has just begun to tap possibilities which in relation to eighty million of people are almost boundless. Sugar, which years ago was too expensive to be lavishly consumed by the well-to-do, now freely gives its heat to the workingman. It is more and more advantageously used as a strength builder among the underfed. The demand that will follow the developing taste for it can be met by the vast quantities latent in Porto Rico and Cuba, and beyond them by the teeming lands of South America, and beyond them by the virgin tropics of another hemisphere. Tomatoes, the hot-house delicacy of the Civil War time, are doing now what many a bloody revolution failed to accomplish: they have relieved the monotony of salt pork and boiled potatoes upon the poor man's table. The clear acid flavor of the canned vegetable lightens ugly heaviness, and adds tonic gratifications for the lack of which men have let each other's blood. The tomato will grow on ground inhospitable to other cultivation, it needs little care either on the vine or in the cannery, and the ease of marketing it, together with the enormous demand, have worn the price rapidly down to eights cents a can for the poorer brands. The "specials" offered by cash groceries at seven, six, and five cents extend the circle of purchasers, and the poor man's wife finds their ragged contents very satisfactory when served with her dull meat stew.

Within the last decade the concentrated food value and the delicate flavor of green peas have been added to the dietary of the workingman. The former high prices have been reduced to nine or ten cents, and the primeval barrenness of Colorado, reclaimed by irrigation, has scarcely begun to yield a quota of its crops. Irrigation permanently fertilizes land, and by quickening growth gives richer flavor to vegetables. If these advantages keep the prices of desert-grown vegetables above those the poor man can pay, the varieties now ranking best will descend to his uses. The preservation of food by canning is to time what transportation is to space. One opens an indefinite territory and the other secures an indefinite time in which to consume what has been quickly perishable. The easy and almost unnoticed fall in the demand for meats during the recent beef-trust scandal shows that meat is not the standard of life in the sense that bread was in the eighteenth century, and that a plundering tax can never again involve the poor in hardships comparable with those formerly laid upon the English by salt and wheat imposts. In America, meat three times a day permits monopoly, twice a day high prices, once a day it means cheapness and plenty; for if we are convinced that meat is the staff of life men use this belief to build an artificial monopoly upon. If meat is relegated to a coördinate place in a well-ordered diet, it must become as cheap as bread and potatoes.

In the specific instance of rumored scarcity and famine prices during a late strike, the workers were by no means seriously affected. The Russian Jews turned without much ado to the fish they had depended upon in Russia but had discarded here because it was less fresh than it had been in their river towns; and the Northern meat-eating stocks, like the Germans and Irish Americans, increased the consumption of coarse vegetables by putting less of the cheap tough cuts of beef into their stews. Salaried people and the higher class of laborers felt the embargo more than the vast majority of immigrants who have not yet learned to measure their well-being by the pounds of flesh they consume. A vegetable diet is normal to the Italians and semi-tropical people, and the result of a protracted strike or a packer's monopoly will probably be the loss of a potential market without detriment to the health of South Europeans in America. The development of meat tastes, it is not perhaps too much to say, will depend upon the ascendency of Anglo-Saxon tradition rather than upon the needs of modern men, who are adequately warmed in their homes and protected from extremes of weather while outside them.

Rapid distribution of food carries civilization with it, and the prosperity that gives us a Panama Canal with which to reach untouched tropic riches is a distinctive laborer's resource, ranking with refrigerated express and quick freight carriage. The produce which the railroads bring to cities have made ice a commonplace of the larder. Without it milk would cease to flow into New York from Adirondack farms four hundred miles away; it opens a market for fresh fish to people who have hitherto eaten it only in oil or in a dried form; it gives options upon the winter's market as well as upon the summer's, and adds many perishable fruits and short-lived vegetables to the laborer's menu. In the Philadelphia ghetto one may watch a huckster's wagon, filled with strawberries costing three and four cents a box, move down the block and go away empty on a day when a box uptown is not to be found at less than ten cents. Other wagons offer lettuce, celery, corn, and spinach banked crisply against the blocks of ice in the wagon bed. Banana carts make their rounds during the whole year with excellent fruit for ten and eight — and late on market nights for six — cents a dozen. The consumption of bananas among the poor is very large; it may be said to have become a staple without regard to previous food customs because of its small waste, its solid nutriment, and its low price. Like sugar, the banana can never again be a luxury; its simplicity and economy of preparation and its compact food values have added it permanently to the laborer's fund of goods.

It is the worker who reaps the advantage of food bargains not to be found in stationary shops. The huckster whose expenses are low offers his wares late at night and calls to the windows many purchasers who have waited for him and are ready to take advantage of the exigencies of ten o'clock. The daytime commissary of the streets, spread on stands and hawked from baskets, also feeds the children more delicately than they were fed in their fathers' countries. Much is unwholesome, much is adulterated, but the food is unstintedly there, and plenty does not fail. It is but natural that a badly ordered menu should be one of the first results of the bedecked and festival appeals to the palate that are made to growing young people and the newly arrived immigrant. Periods of excess in unaccustomed "fancy things," like two-cent glasses of soda water, cheap candy and cake, alternate with periods of undereating. The disorganized dietary, in fact, frequently persists for several years in families which are on the bare subsistence level. The reason of it is illustrated by the judgments two factory girls exercised on the way home from work one afternoon. They found themselves hungry and decided to dine as they walked rather than wait for the home fare or the coffee, cake, and ice cream of a settlement club dance in the evening. They bought rye bread sandwiches of strong mustard and two frankfurter sausages, and quenched their thirst with chocolate soda at the next street fountain. They then ate strawberry and coffee ice-cream, and being still unsatisfied, completed their supper with a chocolate éclair. They spent twenty cents each and were so satiated with sweets that they refused the refreshments at the dance.

The confusion that has followed the breakdown of old dietary customs is now being corrected, in a measure, by a number of social agencies which attempt to bring order by systematic instruction in dietetics. Settlements and training schools give cooking lessons to mothers, children, and young women, in which substitutes for meat are carefully demonstrated and the cost of each dish computed. Many of these courses are simple and practicable and will accomplish their ends. Palatable lunches served in the public schools by semi-philanthropic societies, food and health exhibitions, restaurants and dining-rooms opened by social capital, and the steady advice of kindergarten teachers upon the food sent from home for the children — all these methods are adapting the rude bulk of our prosperity to individual instances.

Beneath this admirable superstructure, however, lies the potent basic fact of a civilization whose bounds are indefinitely widened because the unskilled laborer need be no longer held to the plane of sheer animal terror by uncertainty of food and employment. Artificial culture and experimental science have already fundamentally altered the elemental relations existing two hundred years ago between population and environment. Yet to say that the methods which have made men physically independent of the local food supply are artificial, is to underrate the powers of the new forces by implying that they are constantly opposed by fundamental natural forces which in the end must again triumph. The final victory of man's machinery over nature's materials is the next logical process in evolution, as nature's control of human society was the transition from anarchic and puny individualism to the group acting as a powerful, intelligent organism. Machinery, science, and intelligence moving on the face of the earth may well affect it as the elements do, upbuilding, obliterating, and creating; but they are man's forces and will be used to hasten his dominion over nature.

Each gain upon nature adds to the quantity of goods to be consumed by society and lessens the labor necessary to produce them. In one form the surplus is stored in individuals as surplus energy; in another it is in the goods produced by this energy. Goods become utilities in consumption, utilities are transformed into energy, and energy as work creates new goods. The surplus is not conserved as a permanent fund, but exists and grows only as it is perpetually transformed from goods to energy and from energy back to goods. Life, work, and happiness are thus bound together and their measure is the surplus that vitalizes them. It relieves the present from the menace of a deficit which our forefathers constantly faced and feared. As a concept of our social thinking it differentiates the new from the old and helps to drive away the mists that blur clear thinking. But states of mind are hard to change, and in truth those we so long ago adopted seem to find ever fresh justification in the evils which remain to afflict men long after their inciting causes have disappeared; and in the old wounds of humanity it is easy to see new proofs of accustomed beliefs. The strongest arguments can be presented just as their foundations are crumbling to decay. We know that the military state is gradually being displaced by the industrial state, and yet there never was a time when the power and efficiency of armies were as great as now. They hold the nations in their power just when the disintegration of the forces beneath them is most apparent. And so it is with the evils more directly associated with the industrial world. The poverty, misery, exploitation, oppression of the poor; the greed, indifference, and power of the rich, are glaring truths even while the basis of a new economic order becomes more and more plain. In the age of transition the old thought and the new world abide side by side. But if the foundations of our civilization have been changed, the altering status of men will take clearer aspects in each new age, and the old thought, while apparently verifying the old premises anew, will gradually disappear — not because it is argued away, but because men's sentiments are changed by new activity and an accumulating store of fresh experiences.

CHAPTER II

THE BASIS IN HEREDITY

CHAPTER II

THE BASIS IN HEREDITY

A SURVEY of physical resources shows a world generously furnished for man's comfort. We cannot accept the assertions of the eighteenth-century theologians that this is the best of all possible worlds; but we must admit with the modern physiographers that the materials for humanity's rapid development are ample. We must also join the critics who say something is wrong with a world where men have advanced as slowly and uncertainly as they have since their history has been recorded. Five thousand years are a short span, but we know that a steady normal evolution ought to have borne men further than they find themselves at the close of the epoch. No truth confronts us more baldly than this, that periods of decay and reaction have interrupted those of life and construction. The failure to find a sound basis for civilization is tragic enough to overcome the most courageous with the scourging fear that the instability of social structures is the result of some fatal defect in the constitution of the earth itself. But we look for the causes of the obvious failure in too narrow a field, being confined in the search by a faulty training and a distorted educational tradition that is bound to bring forth unsound theory. Because discouraging economic effects have followed historical struggles to erect permanent civilizations, men have concluded that the causes of the disasters are economic also, and have formulated a series of rigid and exclusive laws which apparently explain the processes of racial disintegration. These laws seem firmly knit when they are interpreted upon an historic background of moving pictorial events; but when they are stripped of their setting, they cannot withstand the geographical and purely economic evidence presented by the world as it now is. Some vital factor has been overlooked by those reasoners who use accepted formulæ to explain society.

Of late, however, men have begun the task of isolating the neglected truth that causes increasing variance between fact and theory. And they are finding it in the force of Social Heredity, which has wrought from past conditions a psychological environment that exercises power side by side with its twin force, the material environment of to-day's soil, food, and climate. Social heredity is experience transmitted from the distant past, influencing men independently of the economic environment, which is the sum of contemporary experiences.

THE BASIS IN HEREDITY

Men's minds are generated, moulded, and restrained by a realm differing from that formed by the physical features of nature. The mental habitat embracing the social inheritances of the race is for a long time, in a new environment, the real centre that interprets and modifies purely physical conditions. Races are constantly changing their economic medium by migrations or by improvements in local circumstances, and they develop in each period social institutions and mental reactions which remain effective instruments long after the environment itself has vanished. The slow accumulations of customs, manners, and habits of thought flow with increasing power through well-established civilizations and often determine men's progress or their failures more decisively than the forces rising from direct relations with nature. When a poor and static population occupies a rich dynamic region, the cause of the maladjustment will be found in its social inheritances. If fishermen from Labrador should colonize an Illinois corn region, the poor crops and unhappiness that would be recorded by their historian ought not to be attributed to economic causes; the institutions of a Northern fishing folk would be the sole hindrances to rapid evolution. The reasons why the Southern negro has not established an agricultural civilization are psychological and in no sense economic. Men who have lived in a

D   [33]

fertile, smiling land become fearless, independent, and impulsive; those who live in difficult places are cautious, and have a keen sense of comradeship and the values of self-subordination. If a people having the qualities derived from dominion over nature and the satisfaction of wants — qualities which may be called economic — should change places with another whose traits have been formed by long struggles with harsh circumstances, — and are therefore social, — the results of the exchanges could be truly analyzed only through the contrast of racial characters.

Our social inheritances come from two radically different forces that have been acting upon us from the first. One springs from universal deficit — the poverty of the early world; the other emerges from the later store of goods which build the social surplus. The bonds uniting the first societies were made by wars, famines, irregularity of supplies, and the other causes of common primitive poverty, which forced men into groups that could survive the reign of want when the free individual must have perished. The dread of foes and the craving for sympathy in disaster bound men together even while immediate economic advantages might have called them apart. Terror and suffering developed social solidarity long before men were intellectually able to conceive the economic values of coöperation.

On this groundwork was constructed the social unit like the horde, the tribe, and the clan, contingent upon deficit and aggregated by fear and pain. But at the same time was thriving the normal evolutionary unit of the biologic family of father, mother, and children. Such an organization, renewed in each generation and in no sense representing a property holding line of descent as it later came to do, was effected by a surplus of strength within the individual. The children of parents with scanty resources developed too rapidly and supported themselves too soon. But when the adults were vigorous and well-fed, the family became more compact, and the enormous advantage of prolonged childhood began to accrue to the race. With increasing definiteness the man has continued to give his muscular strength to the service of wife and child; with minuter specialization she has stored her physical surplus of milk, of intelligence, of strength in tissue and bone, for the uses of her young; and the child has remained helpless longer that it might serve more adaptably in maturity. The extended period of care gives to the protected greater flexibility of mind and plasticity of body; to the protectors it yields a higher specialization of function, and a coördination of the mental and physical halves of being. Prolongation of childhood has united the family in the same way that war, want, and uncertain income united the larger group. It was necessary in both cases that the strong should acquire a surplus and be willing to devote it to the young and weak; physical modifications enabled them to accumulate such an excess of energy, and mental modifications rendered them willing to use it for the greatest general good. Adaptations were thus brought about which gave men a heredity containing the qualities of sympathy, mutual aid, and self-sacrificing love upon which group and family life depended and which utilized the growing physical reserves. If the surplus is taken away the family disintegrates; in a dynamic society where free opportunity is given for the prolongation of childhood and the play of the caretaking qualities upon helpless, irresponsible young, it becomes a firmer and more valuable integer. In a world without poverty it can be relied upon as the natural mechanism of the evolutionary process.

But the unification of interests, and the consequent hastening of evolution which it could have brought about, was disturbed at the dawn of civilization by a change in the form of the stored wealth. In the course of time the general level of poverty was left behind by men who appropriated more and more of the common store, and their possession of it generated ideas and institutions in opposition to those of the masses on the poverty plane. A large and old surplus, after it has served as the primary means of bringing a society into cohering order, gradually replaces altruistic traits by selfish and short-sighted qualities in the men who control it. Nomad tribes amalgamated into the agricultural nations of grain lands; in upland regions clans blended to protect their cattle; and swelling aggregations of men produced a residual supply of goods that freed them from the worst perils of nature. But the reserve of wealth drew them into fratricidal contests for its possession, and when one race had conquered another, enslaving it for a long term, normal evolution was interrupted and an unnatural status fixed. The abnormal formation of aristocracies first roughly stratified society when upland races conquered lowlanders; and everywhere in human history an established position and competency in nature has made it possible for the stronger to divert the economic uses of the weaker to themselves. The biologic differentiation of functions within the group united by common interests has been disturbed by the alignment of group against group and a savage exploitation of the defeated. The tribute-takers and the tribute-givers in some of many forms follow the appearance of the social surplus. Women were quickly forced to render economic and personal service to men instead of being left free to care exclusively for the children. Then came the military and priestly classes, who oppressed and terrified the poor; the leisure classes, who robbed workers of their surplus; the cultural classes, who believed themselves the ordained superiors of the less lettered and held themselves fastidiously aloof from the majority of their fellows; and the successful families of the modern commercial and producing classes, who readily acquire the characters and customs of the ancient aristocracies. All of these successive types have been true aristocracies, in that they place the preservation of their class above that of the race. They have not been producers of wealth in the modern use of the term, and have, on the contrary, scorned production or been indifferent to it, regarding it as the function of the "servile class." The conquered man has been controlled by the man with the surplus until it has come about that the poor are born on one side of a line and the aristocrats are born on the other. From their birth, some move toward an unearned share of wealth and some to unmerited want; the contrast between the surfeited and the exploited is never blotted out. Free access to young democracies and virgin countries does not obliterate it, for heredity gives to the newcomers ancient social emotions in which all share, either as instinctive aristocrats or servitors. The aptitudes for service and sacrifice like loyalty, meekness, timidity, and distaste for strife, fit men for the congregate activities of shop and home, but make it easy for the self-centred aristocracies to seize the social surplus and so confine the defrauded men to the ancestral status of poverty.

There have flowed then, side by side, two streams of life, one bearing the working poor, who perpetuate themselves through the qualities generated by the stress and mutual dependence of the primitive world, and the other bearing the aristocracies, who dominate by means of the laws and traditions giving them control of the social surplus. The poverty instincts common to all in a universally niggardly environment belong now to the modern workers whose position on the edge of subsistence has made them continue to meet like situations with like safe-guarding qualities. They survive by means of natural characters that appeared in the animal world, and reappear with augmented influence in all peoples forced to depend upon each other for safety and race continuity. The long lines of aristocracies over against them are not connected by physical descent. Each new one has sprung from the primeval stock of its region, the bond with its predecessor being not one of blood, but of inherited customs and culture. Civilization is a self-perpetuating tradition, but it has not yet given men a self-perpetuating heredity. The line of race continuity runs through the poor, the sequences of property and institutions through the rich. The traits that distinguish them are not additions to the sum of characters possessed by all mankind; they are the effect of a suppression of universal character showing itself on different groups in different ways. Classes are not differentiated by an increase in the number of their qualities, but by the inactivity of certain ones brought about by the lack of conditions that will exercise them. It is necessary to contrast the human nature expressed through the medium of a social class with the human nature it suppresses before the real and complete heredity of the race can be known. Class qualities represent losses, not growth. Take certain ones from the total and a group of men become aristocrats; take others and the middle class appears; select others and the typical man of poverty passes sadly across the stage.

These results of suppression will be seen more clearly when they are related to their causes in surplus and deficit. Wealth and want oppose each other in their influence upon human nature. Riches sate desire and stifle impulses with lethargic fulness; chronic want, starved desires, and dwarfed impulses render many of man's faculties inert. When poverty continues long enough to affect children, the period of infancy is shortened, maturity is correspondingly hastened, the unfolding of the higher faculties is arrested, and the race reverts to a more primitive type. Children robbed of the treasures of their race heredity by child labor or by the poverty of their parents show qualities in adult life which are only the defaced remains of what generous human nature implanted within them and would have developed under favorable circumstances. The "man with the hoe" is produced by a suppression of the material which is quick within those who despise him. The general differences between classes may be summed up by saying that satiety quenches the emotions while prolonged want enfeebles and distorts the imagination. The loftier emotions were evolved by group action to cope with pressing evils. Sympathy, friendliness, courage, love, have come to noblest fruition in races hard beset by persistent foes and circling perils. Conquer them, satisfy concrete needs with abundant riches, and the stimulations of the elemental instincts and energies of the race become less and less until they no longer spur to action. A plethora of riches acting upon a group for generation after generation smothers many fundamental characteristics common to mankind; and the apparently new qualities of leisure people are but remnants of the nobler individuality that would flourish in a natural environment. Assured wealth also overdevelops in its holders the secondary and less essential traits until they become insignia of inherited luxury and culture that interfere with the activities upon which the survival of other classes depends. A laborer with a small, soft hand would be unfit, a working woman with a frail waist would be handicapped, but weak hand and waist may be safely cultivated by the rich as marks of distinction, accentuating the differences between wealth and want. It must be reiterated that the unlikenesses are either suppressions or real degenerations of character. Aristocratic activity and sumptuary idleness have not yet added one valuable trait to the stock of the working poor. The lord and the lady have not surpassed the coachman and the maid in character development; and their objects of pride represent what they have lost since their ancestors left the common road and what their servants could not lose without being discharged.

While the weakening of stimuli is clogging the primary instincts of the leisure rich, the poor degenerate under the throttling of want. The faculty of imagination is fed by the surplus energy of individuals; it dwindles when there is no tide of free energy to lift it above the monotonous courses of the present. As long as the few imperative demands made by hunger, disease, and stagnant misery absorb the mind there is room neither for far-ranging, loftier ideas, nor vitality to conceive them.

Terror is the one source of fancy which then brings forth suspicion, deceit, and superstition to master the mind, distort the vision, and debase the thinker. Students of the poor classify these rank offshoots of fear as elemental characters developed in the blood, and conclude that only a long period of evolution will destroy what is in reality a short-lived product of the unwholesome food, bad air, debilitating climate, and other preventable conditions that rob men of vigor and of forethought. Abolish poverty, transform deficit into surplus, fill depletion with energy, and the ascribed heredity of the poor will vanish with its causes. No slow elimination of characters need precede the transformation of the servile man into the straightforward, fearless comrade. His essential characters are not manifest in him as we see him; they are revealed by those descendants of earlier poverty men who have broken the bonds that held them in want. Their constructive imagination, their foresight, their emancipation from superstition and fear, will be his also as soon as he is lifted from his quagmire. He is what he is, not through lack of character, but through the suppression of it. A steady surplus will do for him what it has done for workers who have long experienced ease and enjoyed their security in nature. Nothing but the rise of the masses to a plane above uncertainties of income can give to society an improving, stable, physical heredity. Then the old traits will give way to a series springing from economic plenty and industrial freedom. Already the gulf between social and physical heredity is visibly narrowing, and there emerges a new social unit differing from the first one founded on deficit, and from the second founded on the surplus within the small isolated family. It is the coöperative group, evolving upon a basis of the surplus stored by coöperative effort, and reëstablishing the biologic family with a lengthening period of childhood.

CHAPTER III

THE BASIS IN FAMILY LIFE

CHAPTER III

THE BASIS IN FAMILY LIFE

POVERTY ought to be disappearing from a rich and lavish world; but it flourishes, and we may well seek the reason for its vitality among the social institutions which originated in earlier conditions of rigor and are vehicles to carry on the habits formed there. The institutions of the present are the modified relationships of the past established during pervasive and all-powerful poverty. The family remains the least changed and retains, therefore, the most direct connections with the old economic foundations of existence. A man's religion and politics have a remoter bearing than formerly upon his food, shelter, and comfort. Matters of belief have ceased to affect the broadened channel of supplies into which he may now dip without hindrance by prince or priest; but his family status continues to relate him to the primary wants in the fundamental dependence upon income and outgo. The family, in its social aspect, was a device evolved for protection against danger, for advantage in toil, and for race continuation. The tie was made by poverty, in

poverty; and it is still taken for granted that the poor
will marry, while it ceases to be equally natural that the
strong shall exact tribute or that nations shall go to
war about a point of kingly honor. Family life is the
physical complement of social conditions in a way that
no other human arrangement can be; but it may become imperfect by a hardening of its forms, and man's
reactions to nature may be so incomplete that marriage
operates to sustain the miseries of poverty rather than
to overcome them in correspondence with its first function. The modern poor, whose experiences most closely
approximate those of our ancestral type, create families
at the edge of want; but they cannot long succeed in
perpetuating the race thereby, because such a group is
not equipped with the ideals and resistant forces which
will withstand the complex and novel perils of urban
life. It is as if the structure of the biological unit
of father, mother, and child should remain perfectly
adapted to the purposes of nature, while the intellectual
principle, whereby it seeks to fulfil its ends, was falling
into decay — as if its intelligence should be at fault,
leading the organism to defeat through its failure to
take heed of the future in its instinctive exercise of the
precautions of the past. Race preservation must follow the line of greatest safety; that is, men must have
confidence that the protection they devise for the con-

tinuity of the species shall not give way. They found security in prehistoric days, as their animal ancestors had been taught to find it, in the family as a social or self-sacrificing unit devoted to race duties at any cost to itself. World poverty made the necessary motive of social subordination stronger than the opposing self-expressive or purely economic motive which would have impelled the members of a family to move independently toward their immediate and individual advantage. The poor survived by ceaseless surrender and were safe because they had only life to lose, and their lives were valuable to their masters. Native warriors and foreign invaders purposely spared them to work. Population after population passed over the toilers as they passed over the fellahs of Egypt. The poverty men became a permanent order, occupying the static places which lay between the possession of property that would have invited destruction by conquerors, and the deeper destitution which also would have eliminated them. In the wild flux of events about the wealth centres of civilization, the poor at length became the safest vessels of race continuation. The level upon which they maintained their family life was, however, depressed to the lowest possible plane, in order that the bond might hold during periods of great irregularity of resource or of marked loss of

E

control over it. Sacrifice, which was first a biological demand, became a system of conduct, and then a moral derivative of poverty. The aristocracies were quick to take advantage of the inbred tendency of sacrificial service and availed themselves of the qualities it produced to tighten their hold upon the workers and, under social sanction, to exploit them artificially farther than nature herself did. So beset, the family could not have held together without the help of sympathy, which was the grim necessity of sharing food and shelter in order to save life that could not have been saved in any other way. We have long been taught to regard the self-deprivation that has accompanied sympathy as cardinally right, and fresh emphasis has been laid upon the precious quality of self-denial. But suffering and self-denial are merely the obverse of sympathy, the dry husk of social service which does not enrich the world more than ascetics do when they make a pilgrimage with pebbles in their shoes. The principle of sacrifice continues to be exalted by moralists at the very time when the social structure is being changed by the slow submergence of the primeval world, and the appearance of a land of unmeasured resources with a hoard of mobilized wealth.

But in spite of the formal teaching of another era, the comparative freedom of access to movable riches which

the workers are securing weakens the sacrificial motive
and frees the repressed economic impulse to serve as
the more suitable instrument of a new order of things.
In young and poor societies the principle of self-subordination and surrender extends from the person of the
mother, who expects to bear and rear a family at all
costs, to the wage-earning shoulders of the father, who
accepts heavy economic burdens at great cultural loss
to himself and to his type. But the industrial movements of the twentieth century are inducing the poor
away from the country, where they knew well how to
cling to the poverty levels of an accustomed habitat,
into the cities, where the line of race security wavers
beneath untried conditions. Difficulties in towns are
too massive to be surmounted by the altruism of such
service as can be rendered by the mutual aid of family
members and of neighbors. In spacious, pre-urban
days the poverty men of the country had some options
in nature during the seasonal periods of plenty, and
moved with a certain measure of liberty in space large
enough to permit initiative group action. Neighbors
could dam a flooding stream and rebuild a burned
thatch; now, a whole tenement full of people can
scarcely mitigate the colossal accidents of fire and factory. The weight of a city is so great and so constant
that the efforts of a few poor folks to reinstate their

[51]

smitten neighbor are not relatively successful. The family emotion wanes before unfamiliar ills, which united fortitude, sacrifice, and endeavor cannot overcome. Every member of primitive families toiled severely during the periods of stress by famine, weather, and war. But such crushing poverty was intermittent, and in its alternations communities renewed themselves. Now it has become chronic in certain localities where the unbroken round of monotonous work disintegrates the family well equipped with hereditary virtues.

Another untried antagonist with which the poor must battle is segregation with the vicious, the depraved, and the chronic paupers. Formerly they were not exposed to the demoralization of the ill-doers of other classes; their own foibles were distinctive, like their virtues, and the peculiar temptations of those who had been crowded over the poverty line were not thrust upon them under a common roof. The environment of the respectable poor has now become identical with that of the underworld. The poorer the family the lower is the quarter in which it must live, and the more enviable appears the fortune of the anti-social class, which has found a way to easy incomes, to irresponsible extra-marriage relations, and to glittering unwholesome pleasures. The ideals of a personal morality may be no loftier in the agricultural districts of England or in the hamlets of Scotland than they are in the slums of New York: the vital point of difference is that bad living under the older regime does not interrupt physical continuity, while the newer transgressions bring sterility with them. The statistics of illegitimacy show that motherhood follows the lapse of the country girl from virtue, but the city woman knows that she may resort to well-advertised means of evading penalty. The daughter of the farmer or of the village workman may have lived in illicit union with poor men of her own class who could offer her few spectacular pleasures and were unable to save her from disgrace among her peers. If she left her home in shame she served the community as a warning text and guide-post to married virtue, and her children survived in the poorhouses or in her parents' home. In the towns there is no paternity, and if unlawful maternity comes to a girl the stigma may be shaken off at the foundling asylum or by a change of lodging. Paid prostitution seems a guarantee of independence to the factory girl trudging to earn her precarious income; and the gift of a silk dress by a man who meets her as a business superior has barred many a working girl from motherhood. The impact of sparkling street life upon the unaccustomed senses of Jewish and Italian girls breaks the ancient family bonds in the second generation of life in America, and Jewish writers declare that their

[53]

young people are drifting fast and far. The difficulties of those who do not give way to vicious associations are equally serious. The factory system, displacing home industries, takes women out of the house, where formerly she could be a mother and a maker of commodities, and postpones marriage to a later and later period of the woman's youth.

To arouse and reinforce the economic motive of the family, and to use it as a sharp tool in the modelling of a new society, seems to do wasteful violence to the instincts, traditions, and ideals of the old. But nothing is destroyed; no advantage gained through the pains of hundreds of generations need be forfeited by the altered direction of energy moving at the base of industrial civilization. The ethical qualities won by reducing a natural deficit, and by saving the type through the sacrifice of the adult, remain potent in the industrial world — not when the tenement mother lays down her life for her child — but when the spiritual readiness to do so pours itself into activity which creates social riches and adds to the stored fund in which her child may share. Stable wealth, upon which her claim shall be guaranteed by a more equitable distribution, wipes away the old deficit, under the shadow of which the woman blindly builds her family out of her own self-denial. Protected by the social surplus she will marry on reasoned economic grounds, to better her own lot and to secure immediate, mutual advantages by coöperation with her mate. The suffering of the foremothers is made unnecessary by the growth of the surplus. Provision for the future should be made henceforth from the current body of society's riches rather than out of the weakness of mothers; the human being must cease to be the frail yet all-important vessel upon whose capacity depends the progress of the type. World riches may replace the living sacrifice and become the social contrivance that lowers human costs; and we must cease to think that the anguish of the sentient creature is compensated by the development of moral qualities which merely reconcile men to repeating the experiences of suffering. Each generation may spend its current wealth of commodities as formerly it spent the current wealth of womanhood; but Capital in its destruction reproduces itself and passes onward without the deterioration caused by pain. The social surplus is the superlative machine brought forth in the machine age for the quickening of progress. It is an advance upon nature, her waste being saved by human ingenuity at work upon her illimitable resources. We are at the stage of development in which conditions independent of us and scarcely recognized by us are forcing a change from the primitive type of family to some modern or economic form.

Much of the misery of the present is caused by the inability of family life to preserve the urban poor, and by its failure to become a part of a larger group, which alone is able to combat the forces sweeping toward the exposed weak. The reassembled unit must, of course, insure civilization's requisites of survival: complete nutrition, economic choices, protected leisure, municipal hygiene, sanitation, and safeguards from disease. These good things are in opposition to the code demanding submission to poverty; it would be necessary to renounce them if one would live in accordance with the ideals of contentment in one's lot.

But sympathy, pity, and the bent toward service may be used in more extensive and effective ways, establishing the requirements of a higher society by a natural and simple step forward. The old altruism can cope successfully with the new municipal life if the potency of personal service can be increased. Express social emotion through income-generosity as heartily as it is voiced by the devotion of one's person to a cause, and the conditions of poverty will disappear within a generation. Income-service is latent power, and the aid which men can render each other when they secure it is the fit congregate method of attacking the environment. It forces the distribution and rapid circulation of the social surplus; it is a modification and a reinforce-

[56]

ment of morality, and the antithesis of the selfish desire to hoard possessions by individual cunning and legal force. Money releases pent forces, and finds outlet for certain strong yet half-submerged qualities which adapt the family to a larger group. Each characteristic is renewed and readjusted to its work by gradations like those marking the history of mutual aid, which was generated in the animal kingdom, and has taken the forms of civic sense in the patriot and of neighborliness in the tenement dweller driven to bay by tuberculosis or the slack season.

The prolongation of childhood forcibly demands the coördination of the family with a unit of protective power stronger than itself. When an epidemic appears in a tenement, the keenest passion of maternal sacrifice cannot save the children from infection. The individual mother may be taught to fear the typhoid germ, and her devotion to the imperilled child is great enough, not only to make her boil and filter her share of the city's polluted water, but to impel her to walk miles for a pure supply and to go thirsty herself if that would avail; or dazed by exhaustion she will watch night and day beside the bed of the child who dies because it is deprived of impersonal hospital care. The service altruism of such an unselfish mother is unwieldy in its struggle to offset racial depletion; it lacks leaven because it consists of service in kind, and does not have final recourse to expert, departmental, and paid skill. But the income-altruism of the community that installs the municipal filter which saves the child from typhoid, and builds hospitals that overcome the epidemic, adapts the urban type to race ends. It is a social functioning that may become as exact as physiological functioning. Adjustment of the family to the environment is faulty when the housewife is armed only with a broom against the rush of city dirt into her home, and the results are ultimately as bad as if the lungs of her children were faultily constructed. It is an incomplete service if dust is swept into a neglected street, to be sifted into clothing, and swirled back by traffic into unfit dwellings. Although a sacrificial heart may energize each broom, it remains a puny weapon for the safeguarding of the poor compared with the sturdy engines that sprinkle the streets and remove the dust at a fraction of the ultimate cost of one-woman power. In the early days of the social settlement in America, when it was groping for methods, a resident used daily with suppressed abhorrence to push onward with her broom the reeking contents of the gutter. Her hope was that her neighbors would adopt this mode of bettering health, and she believed that the spiritual and practical results of such humble civic service would be reward for the work added to the housewife's day. But her example was too difficult, too malapropos; her effort eddied about and sank under its own weight. Years later, under a policy of aggression rather than one of humble burden-bearing, the settlement persuaded the city to asphalt the street, and it was thereafter kept clean, at the price of war on a corrupt contractor. In the nature of modern things, even if a woman is taught to sweep the gutter, it will not aid her to reach income-power or instil qualities that will give her command over her surroundings. Let proper houses, built by the city or by propertied men, be ranked as of equal importance with the long-established necessity of good cooking, place the poor in them, and the line of race security will be drawn more firmly through civilization.

Family continuity before the era of congestion of populations was not related to shelter as it is now; housing was then a private, independent affair, and it had in the main been let alone in accordance perhaps with the ideal that a home is a castle and its affairs concern nobody but the occupants. The woman in the shelter is slow to leave the base on which a multiplicity of home industries long since established her. She often lags behind men in a slough of confusion and dejection, for the old idealism of which she is the centre has not been penetrated and broken by the imperative necessities that have readjusted man to modern production. Women feel that their times are out of joint, because they are not yet coördinated with the industrial civilization which is penetrating their homes and sifting through their activities.

On the other hand, men's ancient ideals of personal service as the satisfying means of meeting obligations to their country are not greatly altered by the change from military and poor states to non-military rich ones. Their patriotism remains a passionate devotion of body and chattels in time of danger; no personal service is too great to be blindly rendered. But there is no fire in the citizen's blood to illumine the nobility of paying higher taxes. He does it grumblingly, under compulsion, and he fights an increase of the rate with warm determination. Altruism knocks at his purse in vain when the service demanded is of remote advantage. His fellowship is nobly responsive to his physical senses; he will give his time ardently and without pause to a stranger hurt in an accident because he is in a service bond with his neighbor that is ethically perfect and inspiring just so far as he can see him. But the ambulance surgeon arrives and the volunteer is superseded. It is difficult thereafter for the helper to bridge the gap and to project his service across it, where his sympthetic eyes and ears cannot tell him that here is a fellow-creature calling for aid. He does not witness pain, and he has but a feeble intermittent impulse to relieve it in the only way he can when it is beyond his physical presence, — by a gift of money to the hospital. Civilization spares us more and more the sight of anguish, and our imaginations must be correspondingly sharpened to see in the check-book an agent as spiritual and poetic as the grime and bloodstain of ministering hands.

Income-altruism is a moral impulse that may also find precise direction in the life of the poor man as well as in a socializing of the property of the well-to-do. It will impel the sick laborer in the charity ward to contribute to hospital expenses, and in so far give him a stabler foothold in the city than he can find through organized relief. It will make plain to the labor unionist that he serves more effectively by paying dues for a year than he can by facing the police as a picket during a brief strike; and it will make clear to the wife of such a man that she can help more by earning income to pay trained people to divide her labor, to feed her children scientifically, and to educate them, than she can aspire to even by complete self-abnegation uncompensated by wages. The poor need income in order to pay for their quota of care by municipal specialists. If they do not earn it, they are maladjusted to their environment and lose footing in it.

Town poverty is dynamic, moving downward to pauperism and crime in the alluring fields of vice, or climbing upward to economic independence upon fresh opportunities that have aroused the jaded senses. Country poverty is static, propagating itself in a familiar environment by well-worn formulæ. At the same time, excessive consumption of wealth, dissipation, and the vices are destroying successive aristocracies by self-induced exhaustion, and the suicidal group quickly disappears without establishing a line of descent. They continually reform on the old bases and bequeath to society, not sons, but a body of traditions. The present leisure class of America, for instance, is governed by concepts handed down by the Continental nobility of an era that recognized no industrial or business man's ideas.

In the place of these two crumbling bodies — the aristocracies which are being shorn of their powers, and the poor who are thronging into an unnatural dwelling place — is arising the city industrial group. Modern industry has built the city, and towns are therefore the natural habitat of its members. Their position in society is fortified by the social changes that have followed the Protestant Reformation, the French and American revolutions, and English constitutional development. This young class of industrial producers is prepared to maintain itself in a civilization which centres about the city and depends upon work. It entrenches itself most rapidly and firmly in the richest countries, and it constantly calls for more men and women. Its work welcomes workers, and recruits are scarcely subjected to the tests of efficiency so great is the demand for labor. In it may mingle the culture, hitherto solely possessed by the aristocracies, and the physical heredity entrusted by nature to the care of the poor. Leisure and work may supplement each other so fully that every family may have the culture that is the product of the one, and the efficiency that is acquired by the other. The power to work and the power to enjoy will then come to each family through the union of a sound physical heredity and a progressive social heredity. The social surplus will be the inheritance of all, to be used by every generation for the advantage of the next, reappearing as energy with which to improve the race and beautify the world. Then the line of social stability will be the line of family continuity, and there will cease to be an upper and lower class, checking progress by their dissensions. The one enduring institution will be the family, and it will be protected by income and ennobled by service.

CHAPTER IV

THE BASIS IN SOCIAL CLASSES

CHAPTER IV

THE BASIS IN SOCIAL CLASSES

WHEN men look backward upon life they see that death has everywhere been the penalty of peace; when they look within themselves their oldest memories affirm it. Their prehuman experience proved that existence depended upon the ability of a group to keep the subsistence circle around itself free from other food seekers. Then human hordes turned upon each other, and their prowlings about the precarious supplies of food evolved in the course of time into the "wars of civilization." There was little peace where nature was most productive, and the conquering population of the better lands, governing and protecting by conquest, built up whole states on the traditions and practice of fighting. Where civilization developed rapidly, war was frequent and overwhelming; the most highly civilized men were the best warriors, and statesmen and philosophers set forth the necessity and the beneficence of destruction. It was in such a world, where a man's death was his neighbor's gain, that our social institutions were grounded. Men were forced into social groups in order to defend themselves and to control the accumulations of wealth. Predatory habits, which originated in the hunting of game, developed a zest for hunting men as soon as conquests and the possession of slaves made the agricultural resources of valleys more desirable than those of mountain or upland plain. Groups fought so fiercely that the natural passage from one to another was rarely crossed. Each individual had a status to preserve and an income to guard, and relations to nature were lost in the struggle to keep property. The contest evolved social institutions, which do perpetuate and conserve, but which do not improve man's adjustment to nature. Here arises the distinction between the social institutions, which save or dispose of the surplus, and the economic institutions, which utilize both the environment and the labor power in it. The former establishes status and the rights of possession and of exploitation; the other increases mobility of men and goods, promotes industry, and gives each generation renewed power to establish itself in closer relations with nature.

The result of these conditions is two kinds of obstacles that hinder advance. On the one hand are the obstacles economic, maladjustments between men and nature, which forced men in the past to submit to a poverty they did not know how to escape; on the other hand are the obstacles social, which do not originate in nature, but in those past conditions retaining present potency that have aligned men into antagonistic classes at home and into hostile races abroad. The economic obstacles are being slowly weakened by the application of knowledge, science, and skill; but the social obstacles will never be overcome until an intellectual revolution shall have freed men's minds from the stultifying social traditions that hand down hatreds, and shall have given to thought the freedom that now marks industrial activity. Thought must be as mobile as action if social institutions are to be remodelled to serve economic ends by giving to the poor such intense and steady purposes that they shall be lifted from one income-level to another until they are emancipated into their culture rights. The extension of civilization downward does not depend at present so much upon gaining fresh victories over nature, as it does upon the demolishment of the social obstacles which divide men into classes and prevent the universal democracy that unimpeded economic forces would bring about. The social status, properly determined by a man's working capacity, has now intervened between him and his relations with nature until opportunity, which should be impersonal and self-renewed at the birth of a man, has dwindled and become partisan.

If one seeks to determine whether the progress of a given type of man is hindered by a social or an economic obstacle, he will ask: Does he work alone, at first hand with nature, and are his returns commensurate with his efforts? Does he stand squarely up to his environment as a gold miner does in the Klondike, even though his return may be far below the sum of hardship and toil he elects to give? If he does establish voluntary relations, he is not socially exploited. Does he labor at one or more removes from nature like the negro in slavery whose surplus belonged to his owner, or like the free negro who mortgages to-morrow's crop for the use of to-day's wagon? If he does, he is socially interfered with and not poorly environed, for his plight stretches backward into hoary traditions and denials that have unmanned him for a struggle outside his native food-laden forests. The misery-wrung toiler of Millet's picture and Markham's poem is the penalty France pays for ancient class struggles, inherited illiteracy, and congenital weakness. Many single-hearted reformers, like Marx and George, dispute this and have devoted their lives to the proof that the "weight of centuries" would at once drop from the back of the "man with the hoe" and that he would forthwith stand straight if his implement no longer belonged to his landlord but to himself, or if he had not to pay rent from the wretched produce of his stony quarter-acre. They say that he is in the crushing grip of an economic law which operates wherever land or tools are rented as inevitably as gravitation acts where matter is. But he is not to be simply accounted for by a single all-prevailing law; he is the ill-treated child of a long-distant past whom we have never reconciled to the present. He stands as the protagonist of those men who are so coerced and downcast by traditional rulerships that, as Lasalle said of the German proletarians, they do not know that they are miserable. He comes to us from yesterday's wrongs, and he generates beings who are carrying into to-morrow the birth-marks of to-day's evils. Men are moulded into their classes by the pressure of social things accumulating generation after generation, which finally sum themselves into an acquired heredity binding men firmly to their places. The social is at once a record and a continuation of the methods that were necessary in vanished economic environments, telling us how and when economic forces were in action, and its dominance indicates that static are stronger than dynamic conditions. It is with the stratification in human society as it is with geological changes. Existing mountain ranges which divide the world into valleys of varied beauty and width are the effects of forces that to-day are tearing down the huge masses thrust upward by their past activity. A mountain is not a present activity: it is the solid remainder of past forces. Social classes are the product of past situations; and present economic forces, like the active geologic agents of to-day, are tending to level the obstructions raised by their former energy.

Economic forces — if dynamic — should form steps by which men would readily mount from low planes of well-being to higher ones. They should pass out of the single life, through the stage of complete nutrition, and thence into the family life by means of increased income. The freedom and independence of the family ought to be later stages reached by further gains. The era of control, although it is primarily a social influence, has an economic significance in that it marks the point where the ascending person ceases to supply his wants by his own efforts and becomes able to command the labor of others. The lot of the man commanded is depressed or arrested; that of the controller is improved, and the social stratification which interferes with the natural economic progress is begun. Men who cross the line of control enter the military, the aristocratic, the leisure, or the capitalistic class, each of which must be viewed economically because it represents the power to exact service from inferior groups. The middle class are the well-nourished, free, and independent; but complete nutrition, economic freedom and independence are not distinct stages of progress; they have been confused by social pressure until men cannot pass from one to the other by distinct and easy stages into the ranks of the cultured and leisured above them. Finally, there are the poor, depressed so that the line of family continuity has fallen upon that of poverty. They have been preserved as they sink in poverty, and repressed while seeking by natural agencies to reach the levels of the classes that control them.

Thus solidify the strata between the hungry and the well-fed workers, and, again, between them and the groups that hold the power and the culture of civilization. Concealed by the stratifications in society, and often hidden from the casual observer, are the economic forces which, if unobstructed, would build the steps that make progress possible to all. At the left in the chart which follows are the historical classes, and at the right the economic elements which give them being and permanence. The line of poverty marks the minimum below which disease and destitution sweep people away. The line of family continuity represents the smallest income that can hold a family together generation after generation without loss of place and proper traditions. The line of family continuity has been forced downward to the line of poverty by old influences which are still active and cause the exploitation credited to economic law.

THE SOCIAL CLASSES	THE ECONOMIC STAGES
THE LEISURE CLASS	*Line of economic control*
THE MIDDLE CLASS	*Line of economic independence*
	Line of economic freedom
	Line of complete nutrition
THE POOR	*Line of family continuity*
	Line of poverty

This little table, then, is roughly one of antecedents; their consequences exist in society, — not all acting everywhere, or uniformly in given areas, — but some are here and others there, classifying, sorting, impelling, restraining, and themselves in the reluctant flux of change. They have blended into composites whose net results are the three huge social entities that have persisted for thousands of years. The historian is not more aware of the classes than the laborer is, for in the minds of both is a consciousness of the characteristics separating the Ruler — be he soldier, millionnaire, or landlord — from the energetic business man and from the manual worker. Within each group of the diagram the qualities which are continually asserting themselves are determined by the economic position of its members. But no member of the social classes is in direct connection with nature; he is not economically free. Each has his distinguishing traits, his peculiarities of relationship with some other man, which handicap or profit him. The heaviest burden is upon the workers, for they enter family life as soon as they can make an independent fight for subsistence. In European countries the line of family continuity is farther below the line of complete nutrition than it is in America. If the poor of either continent were in direct relation with nature, they would not double their economic burdens until they had established themselves on a more stable foothold than that upon which they adventure now, and had advanced into a plane of comfortable security. But in reality they do: in England and Italy a low-grade laborer marries by routine when he reaches a wage, the equivalent of which a New York laborer thinks barely sufficient for his own support. In Italy, however, a score of instincts, traditions, and inherited qualities impel a man to marry before he reaches the natural level of

complete nutrition. In America the compulsion of ancient social forces soon becomes less persistent, and
young people pertinently challenge the injunctions to
marry before they are in easy circumstances. The religious imperative to increase and multiply, laid down
by nomad Judea's rulers at a time when they knew she
would be enslaved if her warriors were outnumbered,
has become a bar to the progress of industrial Judea
which she recognizes but still suffers under. The ideal
of blind obedience to prince and priest is a social quality
that depresses; it was formerly a kind of goodness like
the mute submission to a great burden. The habit of
renunciation which has been made easier by being
named a virtue has become a social quality acquired
by the poor, not in their struggle with nature, but in
their economic relations with the classes above them.

The traits of poverty, unlike those of the other two
classes, cannot effectively exercise themselves through
the medium of income; they must find their outward
current in personal sympathy, service, and sacrifice.
The middle class is characterized by the ruggedness,
uncouthness, and stern unimaginative strength of men
who act for themselves. They become individualists
working in institutional forms, yet non-coöperatively
because their independence gives them the arrogance
of self-satisfaction. The middle classes lack culture

because they lack contacts; for culture is the perfecting of intercourse with one's group. Economic control means leisure and delimits the plane where amenity, gentility, and cultivation are characteristics acquired by the use of incomes ample enough to command the services of other people. It marks, too, the field where accrues the advantage which the upper class has gained over the other two. Because service is unremittingly given to leisure men, which they have no obligation to repay except with the market wage, they are selfish beneath the urbanity and ease that lend beauty to social forms. The three lines, Poverty, which means anxious uncertainty and irregularity of income, Independence, which means crude and happy well-being, and Leisure, which is the fine flower of others' efforts, cannot coincide, being opposites and divergents, not made by the resources of nature into which all may dip, but by the social antagonisms of the unlike.

Their relationships upon which depend the income of each, fixed as rent, profits and wages, are treated, however, by the majority of people as the functioning of pure law emanating from a remote province of nature. The "Iron Law of Wages" is feared and hated as the fiat from some far Economic Kingdom which imposes ordinances upon society as nature has laid the commandment that rain shall follow precipitation. But as we watch the Iron Law shift and change through the centuries with the changing purposes of men, it ceases to be law and becomes the crystallizing record of inherited submissions and of weakness too weary to struggle. Nor is the "Law of Rent," so graphically described by Henry George, of super-social origin: if some new quality should emerge and make our children believe that men cannot bargain for land more justly than they can for human slaves, what "law" would then reduce wages by lowering the margin of production? Should we wish to know how an economic force operates and observe the influence of pure economic convictions upon men, we would have to discard historical classifications. The outline of the new relationships would resemble this. See page 79.

Heredity, and the traditional and spiritual factors like religion, patriotism, and the desire for family life have been suppressed in this picture in order to emphasize the material, local, and temporary conditions which are economic. That done, the line of Family Continuity becomes coincident with those of Economic Freedom and of Complete Nutrition, because society would be directed by immediate desires and the motives of the moment in place of the long-continued pressure of group ideals and ancient axioms of conduct. Men would decline to marry at the cost of comfort and of independence, and women would also refuse while marriage destroyed their income-valuations. Poverty, the penalty of losing place in social relations, is at so many removes from nature that it is omitted from the diagram. The young men would be educated and maintained as future producers until they had the capacity for economic freedom. The motives to marry would no longer be planted by the priest or monarch or any other extra class influence; the impulse to it would be native and natural.

THE SOCIALIZED CAPITALIST

The line of economic generosity

THE DOMINATING CAPITALIST

The line of economic initiative

THE FARMER
THE SMALL CAPITALIST

The line of economic independence

THE WORKMAN

*The line of economic freedom and
the line of family continuity*

DISSOLUTION

Aside from the poor who are the most artificial and falsified of groups, we find that succeeding strata in actual society are decreasingly influenced by outside classes; and therefore the economic types of the chart do, in fact, move in an economic direction within the organization of to-day. There is also a new class on a fresh economic base which is attracting much critical attention in America. It is composed of the hundreds of thousands of workers who have reached with a bound the line of full nutrition, the way having been cleared for them by the insatiable demand for men to handle the inrushing wealth of America's resources. Placed in a young, industrial civilization, their advance has been so swift and urgent that social restraints have fallen from them; they have broken old habits of fealty to bonds; they have forgotten the sympathies that made good service to employers a virtue to be sought, and they have not attained new industrial traits that make work enjoyable. They have been changed from drilled and dutiful beings to raw recruits of an economic freedom, which to them is complete because in the exercise of it they for the first time gratify their wants and keep pace with their material desires. Their employers and other observers characterize them as having an unreliable, undisciplined independence in their industrial relationships, — these half-skilled mechanics, grocers, clerks, butchers, barbers, household cooks, domestics, and the rest of the army of the wasteful, ineffective, and indifferent. It is said of them that they render unsatisfactory service and shirk the equivalent of their wages because they can find new places with less effort than they can do their work in the old ones. They are generally inefficient, yet always in demand, unskilful, yet reasonably sure of employment; and thus fortified they have become the peripatetics of industry. Their obvious value to society gives them an independence which is not justified by their power of initiative, and a mobility which is without thoughtful far-seeing purpose; they have fallen into a period of arrest because they are satisfied with a status in which their gratifications are flush with their wants. They are for the moment without motives to work well; in the first place they "owe nothing," they say, to the chance stranger who bespeaks them, and in the second, their conscious and simple needs are so amply met that reasons for working well are lacking.

Of this class was a woman who took a position as highly paid cook in a family of two. When she proved to be frankly untrained and incapable, and was taxed with false pretences, she said with hurt dignity, "You got a pair of hands to wash some of your dishes for you, and I've seen ladies waiting a long time for that."

A similar necessity for services was appreciated by a
barber who came an hour late to the shop. The chairs
were filled with impatient customers and his employer
asked in a mild aside, "What ailed you this morning?"
The young man replied with audible bluster, "Thank
God, I don't have to take impudence from anybody,"
and walked out of the door. In the course of a year
the patron of the vegetable, fruit, and meat markets of a
great city notes how the employees change. "They get
restless after a little while in one place," said an employer. "For the last few years I haven't counted on
keeping the ordinary fellows more than six months.
I just let them go and take the next one who is always
dropping in." The general conviction of security is
only less in degree than that of the economically
complacent chambermaid who anticipated a richly
merited criticism by saying, "Madam, I assure you I
could just cross the street to-morrow and be paid as
much as you give me." Selfish, satisfied, and capricious,
these young people newly emancipated into economic
freedom are seldom idle; they work, but they are marking
time on the spot they have reached, for they do not perceive any options desirable enough to lead them beyond
those they are now enjoying. This is the rich and prom-
ising truth of a situation which is so confusing in its tran-
sitionals that many sympathetically recognize as their

own the discouragement of a just and generous woman who said from her years of experience, "High wages won't improve them; presents don't tempt them; blame doesn't mortify them, and praise doesn't attach them."

Far beyond this tumultuous young group is another which has also recently become economically distinctive in American life. Passing the earlier stage of adjustment between men and wealth which was formerly marked in this country by farmer and landowner, it contains as its type the man whose well-being, greater than that of the farmer and shopkeeper, has inspired him with confidence to initiate vast new businesses, and to remodel, correlate, and aggregate old ones. He pioneers, reorganizes, and ultimately he dominates. He is self-centred and indifferent to the effects of his plans upon the happiness of others. He reorganizes men for purposes frankly selfish; as scientist, explorer, or entrepreneur, he exults in work and in lordship over nature. His relation to society is that of the agent who increases its returns and governs its energies. As a captain of industry he patrols the vast wealth of his class, and he is openly proud of his personal accumulations. When men of this class confront their environment with consciously increasing power, unhampered by obligations to their fellows, they become specialized, and as the result of that, more individu-

[83]

alistic and unsocial. Their ancient group instincts wane and others cannot replace them. Complete and prolonged freedom with its full nutrition dams the current of early motives, and in their isolation they might stand as the rude models of the "economic man" abstraction neatly drawn by the classicists. Nietzsche, the philosopher, painted such a one in vivid colors. He foresaw the superman as the consummation of a line of freedmen whose selfishness should at length produce a perfect creature unhampered by the drag of his weaker fellows. The personality which is to-day dissolved in compromises with one's group would neither be diluted in the superman by responsibility to his neighbors nor deflected by ends not supremely his own.

These two classes, the careless, insolent workmen and the domineering, self-centred capitalists, are alike in that they have broken the social bonds that curbed their ancestors. Both are clearly economic types, formed in part by the revival of suppressed characters and in part by the action of a rich environment. Many people are shocked when they deal with these results of prosperity, and, smarting under their bitter experience, shrink from further developments of an economic society. They believe they see in the savage antagonisms of these groups a reversion to old struggles on a lowered material plane. On the one side, we are told, are ranged the

Industrial Barons who are more cruel than the nobles of the Middle Ages; and on the other is Organized Labor pursuing its ends as ruthlessly and unsocially as highwaymen do. If the capitalists and laborers were classes in the real sense of the term and in conditions that kept them static, the fear and dislike of them might be justifiable. But they are not classes; they are fluid groups of men passing hastily through the temporary economic stages that replace the older social stratification. The social instincts are part of human nature, and when they assert themselves, these bold individualists will again be brought under control. And the new forces, to which in time they must submit themselves, are not undemocratic passions driving men into distinct classes. Culture and civilization are now beginning to act with economic motives to bring men together. Laborers will feel the spur of expanding wants more keenly after each of their advances, and in order to gratify them they will be forced to accept the discipline of the new industrial régime. In the capitalists the corrective emotion is a generosity that is developing in two forms. The first may be called use-altruism, for it is such paternal kindness as opens private picture-galleries to the public and permits a limited and conditional use of the parks and gardens of estates. In that measure it adds to the fund of socialized wealth. The other sort is an economic

[85]

altruism, a public generosity which is willing to bestow gifts without conditions and to be taxed for public and far-reaching ends. Both kinds grow rapidly; and each capitalizes wealth for social purposes with the quality of future utility. It is this quality which must be lacking in service-altruism. The difference is that which separates the old from the new charity. The one crossed the road to help the Samaritan after he had suffered under bad conditions of highway management; the other patrols the road and arrests the wayside thieves before the traveller falls among them. Service-altruism binds the wounds, breathes forgiveness, and solaces the victims of recurring disasters without attacking their causes. Income-altruism hews to their base, for it has the money power to police and to light the road to Jericho.

When income-altruism has socialized a capitalist and given him stronger motives than the dominating capitalist now has, the cleavage between classes will become less distinct. Efficiency and energy will suffice to raise men from one grade to the next; dissipation and selfishness will eliminate them or drag them to lower levels. The instincts and emotions of all groups will become approximately alike, but will find varied expression as the income changes. Classes will then be made by the power of the increasing income to give industrial qualities to producers or to find for them a fuller expression and better coördinations. But at the present time the effects of social stratification in the form of a leisure class and a poverty class must be recognized as a force determining income. When they are included, the relative economic levels in America look somewhat like this.

$5000	ECONOMIC LEISURE
$2000	ECONOMIC INITIATIVE
$1200	ECONOMIC INDEPENDENCE
$800	ECONOMIC FREEDOM
$500	FAMILY CONTINUITY
$300	POVERTY
	DISSOLUTION

Here are blocked in elementary fashion the income graduations whereby men pass from one stage of progress to another. The dissolution of families in large cities is well-nigh inevitable when its income falls below $500. Those which do cling together are chiefly the latest comers, intruded material which has not yet taken the pattern that their forerunners are adopting. The Italian parents, who landed in New York a year ago, send their ten-year-old boy to work instead of to school, not only because they take it for granted that he must work, but also because they do not grasp the fact that poor boys here go to school. Five years later, when mother and sisters are discomfited by their native dresses and the father wants half-holidays, — when the old social forces have weakened before the advance of new economic motives, — the ten-year-old may still be sent to work. But now there are complaints. "Pietro ought to study Roosevelt-book [history], but padrone is too mean," said a mother, fretfully, herself the daughter of a long line of peasants whose family standards did not include literacy. And now her family living on a dollar a day verges on dissolution; it must move upward toward $500 or downward, where the eliminating forces of prostitution, intemperance, and the other vices sweep it out of the reckoning. The disturbances made by the foreign influx do not threaten a permanent depression; they are but the cost of moving populations over the face of the globe and the clashing of new forces against old ones, which cannot endure outside the condition that generated them.

With $500 the Americanized family can perpetuate itself, balanced by the juncture of depressant social instincts which arrest it below the $800 level, where men without them would be free, and the upthrusting economic motives that would postpone the family until full nutrition were secured. If emphasis is laid, as it ought to be, on the value of the wife's home services in the $500 group, the real income will be estimated at more than the nominal one, and her influence in lifting the members into the next stratum of wants will be as evident here as it is in the succeeding divisions. The computation is based on the money wage of the head of the family and gives no equivalent to the labor services of the wife, which undoubtedly raises the income in goods above the point commonly assigned. In comparing the workingman with the man of economic independence a fair basis of judgment cannot be reached unless a value be given to the unpaid duties performed by the wife, which in other grades of living are provided for from the family purse. A budget of $2000 a year will generally include an item for household services performed by a maid or occasional scrub and wash women. When the work is done by the laborer's wife, she should be credited with a similar item and her influence be noted as raising the standard of family life very much as the presence of a domestic employee raises it. The man who earns $500 and is helped at home by a capable wife, who hangs starched curtains at the windows and dresses her children so that they invite comparison with any neighbor's, certainly has in her services the value of a hundred dollars.

But allowing the amplest margins and making the most of the genuine advance, the line of family continuity remains too low when measured by the sole test worthy a dynamic civilization, — that of physical efficiency in children. Not before complete nutrition, which includes ample and varied food, sanitary housing, well-made and attractive clothing, has been secured by the play of economic choices will the generations be maintained without undue waste at their potential efficiency. By this test we must grant that the families who have less will be pressed further and further downward as civilization advances, until they shatter. The dynamics of the workers is an increased income that will both satisfy and create wants and by doing so will stimulate the hearty unfolding of the life within. And this dynamics is the life and spirit of an economic, unexploited society. Men become mobile and free, and the old social strata crumble forever in the upthrust of new motives. But men will not cease to be social. Economic life will make them more social by reviving the impulses of the primitive world. The new economic man will be like the early social being; dormant qualities will be aroused and economic situation, natural heredity, and acquired characters will advance the race and equalize opportunity.

CHAPTER V

THE BASIS IN SOCIAL CONSCIOUSNESS

CHAPTER V

THE BASIS IN SOCIAL CONSCIOUSNESS

A PERMANENT segregation of the working poor was regarded as inevitable as long as a nation's stability hung upon impassable frontiers, an exchequer filled with gold pieces, and a government administered according to the traditional functions of the Three Estates. Such a world was a *cul de sac* for the weakest, and brought forth in the stronger a philosophic pessimism that has not greatly brightened under the knowledge that civilization, ceasing to be measured by the power of military and aristocratic consumers, begins to be dependent upon the production of goods by homogeneous workers. The basal man of the present is a dweller in poverty as his fathers were; he labors without sharing the immediate profits of his own toil and produces without enjoying his product. He has always been the servant, neither participating in the household life, of which he is an essential tool, nor using the appliances of wealth it is his business to keep in order. In another form he is the pioneer who opens a country, and, like Moses, dies without entering in. He is the woodsman, the miner, the quarryman, dealer in raw materials, and bare-handed wrestler with nature. Again, he is the maker of permanent improvements, an Egyptian slave building pyramids to celebrate victories of which he never hears; a railroad gang laborer laying roadbeds over which he will never ride in a Pullman car; a paver of streets who cannot roll over the smooth asphalt in his carriage. As the army was in military empires, the machine is in the manufacturing age: it is anti-individual, an industrial autocrat, whose caretakers are not free, although they underlie our democracy; they are outside the field of satisfactions, although they feed our desires; they are illiterate and badly housed, although they build the school and the home.

These toilers do not long remain at the margin of subsistence through a fundamental lack of productive energy or because their output is scanty. Their trouble lies in the suppression of natural qualities essential to development, which the stimulating determination of poor people to find fresh opportunities in America is, in itself, sufficient to overcome. The disappearance of old landmarks permits new intercourse and fresh adjustments within the industrial organism; and the consciousness of power excites the younger and more ardent spirits to an individualism that appears dangerous to prosperous men, who are established in their class routine, privileges, and obligations. The young people are venturesome and confident, partly because of the natural buoyancy of youth and partly because the demand for workers between fourteen and twenty-five years of age is more steady than the call for older people, and permits them to roam without restraint over their field, gaining a clearer view of it, sometimes, than wiser men do. They are, as it were, industrial scouts, and their adventures upon the skirmish lines should be awarded a due importance.

The experience of one boy illustrates a situation which has relieved him of fears that beset the poor, and which is spreading the concept of the social surplus among people who have occasion to find employment for the constituency of settlements, clubs, and guilds. The boy's parents, cowed and timid, arrived in Philadelphia from the Jewish pale in Russia. They sent the son to school, where he remained until he was fourteen, a rather morose lad, cherishing numerous grievances. He then went to work, sulkily and doggedly, in a leather goods shop near his home, whence he was soon discharged by the approach of a slack season. He found another place on his first application, and after that for several months he led a life which under his animated

H   [97]

description glowed with life, color, and romance. He left his second position because he heard of a better one in a butcher shop around the corner; but he soon abandoned that from the fresh lust for adventure. The sense that his foot was at last upon the neck of his oppression inflamed his fancies and struck his natural resilience until he believed himself everywhere free and safe. He worked for two weeks in a sweat-shop "to learn the cutter's trade," he naïvely said, and hastened from that, with increasing gusto, to the vestibule of a department store, where he checked umbrellas. Emboldened further, he migrated in the following month to a textile factory five miles north of his parents' known landmarks, and laughed at his mother's fears. When he came home again, having considered the question of his trade in the light of his experiences, he had decided on some form of outdoor life. There was no difficulty in securing what he wanted, and he is now a messenger boy, filling his position capably, the "wanderlust" impulses having been honorably quenched.

It is not surprising, however, that the line of discarded employers trailing behind him should have looked upon him as another failure for whom our country has no place. They designated him to inquiring friends as a "loafer" and a "quitter," who threw away his chances, although they conceded that he was faithful and competent while at work. They frequently added that they had positions available for good workers. They did not suspect that it was the consciousness of their need dawning upon their young employee that swung his mind into wider arcs and gave the spur to imagination with which he drove himself abroad while his father was clinging to the first subsistence-state on which his hands fell when he landed in America.

Many industrial victories like the messenger boy's are being written on the same page as the depressing records of child labor; and it cannot be fairly asserted that the exploiting power is a more significant index of national probabilities than the other force of expanding resource that brings ease of mind and content to the unskilled laborer. In one case the child is overwhelmed by some one's desire for unfair profits; in the other, he is not: and side by side with the evidence of exploitation is evidence that the laborers' realization of their value to the employer is making it increasingly difficult to hire workers with moderate skill or experience. The indifference of incompetents with low standards is one of the causes why they do not advance to steady work under comfortable conditions. It results in confusion and bitterness of feeling against the working poor, because the employing part of society long ago adjusted itself to an excess of workers over positions for them. The complaints and sufferings and meekness of searchers for work seem to be the natural course of things; the crude independence, the churlishness, the rasping manners of the man who suddenly attains the hope of equality, are symptoms of disorder to the employing classes. The protests that follow the approximation of the number of tasks to the number of workers are clearer than those which greet a steady oversupply of labor; employers are more articulate than laborers, and their alarms are more effective than those of the unestablished.

It is class consciousness which inclines us to fear that the million of immigrants annually absorbed in one fashion or another is destroying our conveniences. The crude reasoning beneath it is illustrated by the comments of a housekeeper upon her kitchen and the relation of the general welfare to that institution. An employment agency sent her an Irish girl who had been in this country only three weeks. "I will take four dollars and a half while I am learning," the applicant said. "Do you want me this morning?" The prospective employer made no reply, and the candidate added, "I'll stay with you while I am learning." "But when I questioned her," the housekeeper recounted, "I learned that she came from a mud hut in Ireland, and she had never made a fire in a range or even seen a modern oven before she landed. Yet she wouldn't hear of less than a four and a half dollar wage. I don't know what the country is coming to. I told my husband that when such a state overtook his business too, we might as well go to the poorhouse, since we cannot have our work done for us."

A dearth of workers to uphold the institution of the kitchen meant widespread social disorder to the housewife to whom the natural order would have been a number of equipped candidates from which she might have selected one. The difficult Irish girl was a social burden because she could not fill the specific labor needs of a housekeeper; but several candidates seeking employment would not have indicated social distress. An empty kitchen is the measure of social destitution to one who believes that the home has reached its final form and cannot adapt its functions to labor changes. An overcrowded immigrant quarter, to the man who believes that his country is assuming its definitive forms, is also a menace to the well-to-do. He does not perceive that the tax on prosperity which he pays to mould the raw material into efficient producers, is giving the mass a social consciousness which will eventually make business coöperation possible between the two classes.

The first practical shelter for men just over the subsistence line is a fund for sick, death, or strike benefits, or in building and loan associations. The roustabout reaches a base of civilization when he realizes that he is steadily earning protection by other men, and that his acts are wise. Insurance is a civilizing increment because it releases men from the fear of death without saving rites and an outcast burial in a potter's field. The thought of death without ritual contains for most people a quality of brutalizing horror; and the social tradition that insists upon mortuary ceremonial as proof of status is one of the last to be blurred by the anti-social courses of the criminal and vagrant.

There is in Philadelphia a negro truck driver earning $10 a week who pays a negro insurance society a dollar a week to carry illness and death policies in the names of his three children, himself, and his wife. One-tenth of his income seems to be a heavy tax; but his obvious pride in the regular expenditure, his satisfaction in being a "member" of a business affair, his sensation of well-being behind the bulwarks he has thrown about his family, reduce the charge to moderation. The disproportionate importance he attaches to ceremonial displays and his strong desire to be "buried right" are traceable to African tribal customs; but to more developed men denial of religious forms means the loss of prestige, and to the fully civilized excommunication; so that to the majority it implies living outside a coveted institution in primitive loneliness and dread.

THE BASIS IN SOCIAL CONSCIOUSNESS

Lying beyond the entrance into an intensive and interclass democracy, is a field of social consciousness containing pleasure and political clubs, lodges, secret societies, and labor organizations. Beyond this in a broader area of experimental and idealistic social democracy are the social settlements, the coöperative undertakings, and the societies of meliorists whose object it is to carry the economic and cultural opportunities from one extreme of society to the other. But these steps toward social consciousness are a less comprehensive movement toward unity than modern Industrial Unionism. Utilitarian in its motive, and passionately selfish in its singleness and intensity of purpose, it has a social and ethical significance that is without parallel in the institutions of democracy: it is the first coalition of the economic powers of the basal men and the high-grade, skilled workers. During the last century labor organization could not have been included among the resources available for the civilization of crude masses, because it was not the chief purpose of the leaders of the early Trade Unionism to secure the rewards of his work to the common laborer. The heavy balance of power lay with the labor aristocracy of artisans and craftsmen, the skill of the individual being more valued in European industry than the advantages of the machine process; the craftsmen therefore banded against the levelling encroachments of the more unpractised toilers; and their trades unions were obstacles that served with other forms of class domination to keep the unskilled on a static plane. The philosophy of the early leaders, who limited membership to skilled groups within a single trade and sought to control output by rigorous exclusions, seems comparatively negative in comparison with the positive and constructive theories now directing unionism.

The men who began the opposite movement in America have recognized that the foundation of industrial civilization is being built by unskilled hordes, and they seek to retain control of the ground already won by enlisting all comers in its defence. The unionization of an entire industry and its affiliations in other industries gives them the primary advantage of numbers. Labor leaders say that the best way to lift the structure is to raise the base, and they are willing to insert the lever beneath the lowest stratum of labor. The man who has joined one of the unions formed within the last six years learns that his "lot is bound with that of the whole working class," and "that he can no longer advance by building a monopoly of labor within his trade." The lines of industrial caste must break in order to give the class which has the numerical power free admission into the ranks above it. When the un-

[104]

skilled are a majority within the union, moreover, the advance must be timed by their intelligence and adaptability.

The changes in method which this dominance involves are indicated by the remarkable shifting in the union personnel. The total membership has more than doubled since 1898–1899; but while the old type of union or skilled workers shows a gain of a little more than 50 per cent, the newer group composed of relatively unskilled laborers has had a total growth approximating 300 per cent. The reasons, says Mr. William E. Walling, "are the increasing proportion of unskilled workers in the industry, the decreasing sharpness of definition of the line between the skilled and the unskilled trades, and the greater ease with which the occupations of the skilled can be learned by the unskilled." Within the last three years the American Federation of Labor has marshalled three hundred thousand immigrants under lieutenants who drill them to march shoulder to shoulder behind the American standard of living. Although it is a utilitarian motive that incites the smaller and wiser groups to lead the huge weak one, and a selfish reason that urges them to unify the crowd lest all be involved in rout, there is none the less a spiritual advance. The inchoate and stubborn bands arrive first at the meaning of class consciousness and of its ultimate development into social solidarity; then they are given an educative social discipline; next they acquire an orderly and obedient mobility; and it is but a short step thence to the rights of leisure and of developmental recreation.

The immigrant begins his American life without a clear idea of where or how to find assistance. He is guided more or less by chance and may easily become a permanent victim of the first harsh circumstance. On one term or another, the annual army of hundreds of thousands of emigrant wage-earners find work under subcontractor, boss, or padrone; and whatever the terms, few coherent and persistent protests against exploitation reach the public from the ignorant aliens.

It is at this point that the industrial union, going about its business of standardizing, organizes the men who become as plastic in their hands as they were in their bargaining with capital. After a period of union tutelage they may join in a demand for higher wages or a particular concession, moved not always by a primary cause like personal hunger and wretchedness, but because they have been made responsive to the peril of a lowered mean of comfort to other groups whose language they may not understand, and whose racial enemies they may have been while a mountain barrier bred dissension between them in Europe. When Magyars

— who have been the divergent particles in the race chemistry of the old world — react to the formula "one for all, and all for one" in the coal counties of Pennsylvania, they have been manipulated into class consciousness. On the other hand, when an ideal of welfare has diffused itself through the rough, loose groups, they may formulate demands upon their leaders which in a broad, slowly unfolding policy it is not best to follow. Then explanation, persuasion, and authority are brought to bear upon impatient men to restrain them from an ill-timed attempt to secure a portion of the surrounding stores of wealth.

The constructive citizenship at work in a temperately conceived, long-planned, well-officered strike is as educative there as it is in peace; and in a strike, for the first time in their lives many men experience the difficulties and rewards of representative government. The foremost labor leaders belong to national federations which do not shun responsibility, and their struggles are marked by quiet strategy and diplomatic manœuvring for position. The first days are no longer the climax of exploding passions in men briefly thrown together by spontaneous revolt. There is, instead, something of a holiday air in the orderly and quiet crowds; the knowledge of money in the common treasury gives to the unionist's family and to that of the non-unionist who has been promised a share of it a sensation of reliance upon supplies that breeds self-control and command of temper.

The beginning of the Textile Strike of 1904 will blend in the memories of the boys and girls with long vacation-like days of picnicking and of absorbing stories about what the committees wanted them to do — the committees which sat in daily session devising occupations to soothe irritation and divert the anxieties that lead to violence. A visitor to Fall River recounts that the third week of the "fray" began with the majority of the operatives spending the day at the seashore. Cheerful parties were berrying and clamming; there were still quantities of food available, but families chose to combine thrift with merrymaking and to postpone the appeal to the relief stations. At the end of the first month, when many non-unionists were hard pressed for necessities, the United Textile Workers appointed two-thirds of the Relief Fund to their use; they trusted to the class consciousness of their constituency to uphold them in their support of workers who had never put money into the common purse. The officials went further when they remitted formal levy of assessments upon affiliated unions, and rested the matter of subscriptions upon a voluntary basis. Nor were they indiscreet, for the unions shouldered the responsibility and not only maintained their old averages, but in a number of instances increased their aid. One union which in a former strike yielded $46 under levies sent $100 to headquarters when it was given its will. Another which had paid a three months' assessment of $61 during a previous struggle contributed $100 forthwith and promised the Textile Council $100 monthly as long as the strike should continue.

The recruits of unions, listening to the debates that precede these appropriations, feel a bond tightening between them and their unseen beneficiaries, a fraternal bond which is made plain to them by simple words about joint interests and common safety. They are made conscious of their kind with an understanding of the reasons why they act together which they did not have in Europe, where race hatreds and social feuds, generations older than themselves, segregated them in more or less instinctive groups. In the new world the young man of poverty becomes curious, and questions the source of acts that affect his status. Why does a merchant send a thousand baskets of provisions to the strike headquarters, and what is the relation of that man to the Balkan peasant who eats the loaf? Why does a business association give a thousand dollars to buy food for strangers? What is his claim upon the "organized charity to which he is referred," when his new union comrades cannot aid him? By whose orders does the

Salvation Army give dinners at a strike centre to fifteen hundred women and children? He wonders at the kindnesses not sprung from the traditional obligations of church, village, or blood, and is likely to attribute it finally to sympathy for his ultimate purpose rather than for his immediate plight. He thinks that although his employers and the aristocrats are opposing his struggle to rise from his old servile state, an active public is supporting his attempts to win the suffrage of prosperity.

In the Textile Strike — which was notably free from violence on either side — the system of amusement benefits was used with impressiveness. Certain teams of the New England baseball league played a game for the benefit of the strikers, to which special cars were run; travelling stock companies in Fall River gave "monster concerts"; and gala days were set apart for labor rallies. With the proceeds of these gratuitous services the relief stations were reopened during the seventh week of the strike, converting amusement and jovial play into bonds of good feeling as warm and purposeful as those that common suffering has established. It is through unusual means like these that the weavers have been stimulated to original thinking about social solidarity. Leaders use constructive methods, and pleasant occupations help to solve the problem of discipline which arises as soon as a sense of power gives coherence to loose masses of men. In order that discipline shall be educative, it must be made intelligible and its instruments must be simple and direct. Industrial unionism endeavors to govern men by imposing rules that test but do not overstrain their capacity for obedience. The ignorant recruit is made to understand why fees are required and why a penalty is exacted for non-payment without good cause. On the other hand, when he is brought before a civil magistrate by the city police, a sentence for an unwitting offence seems too often the prick of mere arbitrary power that wakens his hatred of despotism. Public sentiment, which is said to have won the Anthracite Coal Miners' Strike in 1902 and to have lost that of the Chicago Teamsters in 1905, is more and more frequently set up and explained as the code unionists must regard if they would win.

The race has lived in historic habitats that are like a series of concentric circles widening from the small inner areas, safe for the individual, to those successively occupied, when the clan, the state, the nation, the race, and the ethnic type each developed its consciousness of kind. Men lived in the radii of their class protection and acquired a safe-guarding sense of peril as the woodsman acquires a sense of direction; but the sense of peril is as untrustworthy for the men arrested at the edge of

American civilization by their consciousness of Slavism or Czechism as the woodsman's sense of direction would be if he were lost in the streets of New York. Ancient distinctions become confused and meaningless in America, having nothing to sustain them but traditions which are themselves uprooted. The interfering motives and the cross classifications of Europe, caused by the diversity of race, language, laws, and religion, are swept aside for the industrial bond of men, producing and consuming wealth under like conditions of government. The guiding consciousness of the poor ceases to be that of national boundaries and becomes that of economic place. The former is class consciousness based on language, inherited religion, and occupation; the latter is social consciousness resting on economic interests, on product, and on consumers' associations.

The environment of the mobilizing poor stretches to fresh horizons, and they are potentially free to move toward them. They do not know, however, the best ways to avail themselves of mobility. It is in such case that their better located fellows come forward to guide them. They approach the Italians sullenly working side by side but refusing to speak to each other, because their native villages are at immemorial feud, and they wipe away the bootless quarrel by pointing out their identical interests as a new-formed group of American

City Builders. With the new name their minds slowly cease to dwell upon the bellicose traditions of Sicilian towns, and turn toward the whole territory where their union buttons secure fraternal privileges for them. The union card in the coal counties of Pennsylvania mobilizes the bands huddled behind the imaginary barriers of another continent, and moves them about under the one banner of common producers of a single form of wealth. The insignia of labor organizations give men the courage and purpose to use avenues of transportation, sharply reversing the effect of the passport system devised in Europe to be a discourager of movement. Russia hampers her migratory workers as if they menaced the state, and must be handily concentrated and individualized for punishment; in America, Russians stand still instinctively, as if waiting for some new passport to reassure them. Its equivalent is a union card, which brings to the terrorized immigrant a sense of fellowship and of security. The bonds he has known hitherto have been those of locality, parish church, and race. The world beyond his province has filled him with fear and suspicion. It is a great emancipation when he can think in a friendly way of former enemies, and learns that his union is broader in its aims and more extensive in membership than any of the groups with which he may still be affiliated. So he slowly advances

I   [113]

in social consciousness, leaving behind the class consciousness of other conditions, which can now only perpetuate suspicions and arrest growth.

The coöperative spirit has influenced the early formative stages of race development as deeply as the disasters and dangers that brought forth sympathetic aid. Circumstances that demanded coöperation affected the whole group as intimately and continuously as those that made for sympathy; defence was coöperative, so was migration; and their benefits were equally clear to all. There is but one fundamental heredity, and all the natural qualities are part property of the poor. When we observe certain classes like Western farmers reacting successfully through coöperation to agricultural methods which have been too extensive for the old unit to carry on, we have proof that the poor can react successfully to favorable situations.

The growth and influence of cities are renewing and intensifying in all classes the motives to coöperation. Compactness of organization and the obvious similarity of the ambitions of crowded peoples enlarge the units which can profitably work together. Where the manufacturers of one commodity formerly united to market it, trade organizations now promote their city's businesses. The older exclusive trade morality did not condemn ruinous rivalry between a shop and its neighbor; the later inclusive code advocates coöperation against neighboring towns. It is not shop against shop, but city against city. The younger heads of firms talk enthusiastically in terms of municipal and fraternal enterprises. A chief recently alluded to the coöperative spirit in the sections of his large department store. His lieutenants, he said, are interested in drawing people to every part of the plant and in befriending each other. They are united constructively, furthering an enterprise too big to be carried on without strong cohesive power. Cities, like shops, are too great to be managed by small competing units: the municipality wins trade by inviting conventions to visit it, and by giving attractive civic entertainments. A true social unit is thus formed by the coöperation of aggregated interests.

The morality of business and of city enterprises may be said to depend upon the manner in which the coöperative idea expresses itself. The larger groups sway the smaller, setting up codes that eventually become social standards. The democratic and ethical conviction is that the needs of the larger groups ought to have precedence over those of the smaller, and that the public duty of the civic patriot, like that of the soldier, must be done before the private business is finished. The coöperative ethics is loftier than the competitive, which cannot prevent class interests from leading on to fraud and exploitation. Competition solidifies, but coöperation mobilizes and arrests social stratification by assuming the equality of neighbors. The essence of it is: Do for others while they are doing for you. It may even be: Do for them before they do for you, for in this way you reap advantage by being first in generosity. Give a surplus of accommodating deeds and advance a store of commodities so that your neighbor will be under obligations to you. The older trade adage expressed in the parlance of the street is: "Do others before they do you." Individualism and suspicion are the outcome of competition; generosity is a product of coöperation. A Western farmer, growing rich by methods of extensive farming, recently touched upon the new morality springing from a situation too complex to be longer carried on by isolated farmers. "Farming," he said to an old playmate returned after years of absence, "is different from what it was when we were boys. Each farm, you recollect, had then its gang of men to do all its own work, and like as not we were quarrelling with our neighbor about a line fence or stray calves. Now we hire fewer men and we own the big expensive machinery in common. When more men and teams are needed we depend on each other, and we come, too, at first asking! Maybe we have a job pressing at home, but it pays to go. I don't believe a man could get along in this region if he didn't. The other day I saw the man on the next farm tilling his field, and he was behind on ploughing. I said to him, 'Let me plough that field?' 'I see what you want,' he called back. 'You want me to be under obligations to you.' 'That's so,' I said, 'for it is the way to make friends and money.'" The farmer lives an isolated life as long as agriculture is intensively carried on; but extensive farming on a massive scale promptly summons forth the coöperative faculty he has not popularly been thought to possess. His situation reveals a suppressed natural quality. It is a similar situation which suppresses it in the lives of the poor. Give them the leverage of social consciousness resting on class interest, and they will unite to improve their situation as naturally as the farmers, the bankers, the stock companies, and the building associations do.

Their opportunity, however, is rising out of the physical conditions of urban industry, and out of the use of complicated machinery. Massed side by side during the working season, performing similar tasks under conditions which approximate uniformity more closely than they ever have done in the history of workingmen, the simplicity and rewards of coöperative production will soon be apparent to the born leaders of homogeneous bands.

[117]

Government is more accurately representative when each coöperative group trains its leaders, making the successful ready to serve the public in still larger undertakings. As the town meeting is a training in the coöperation of democracy, so are labor organizations, clubs, trade organizations, and all other joint enterprises. Coöperation gives men motives that weaken aristocracy, privilege, and the restraint of business. It is situation *versus* character. Dormant qualities will be wakened by opportunity, and opportunity will make men. As Lester F. Ward has said: "There is no need to search for talent. It exists already and everywhere. The thing that is rare is opportunity, not ability."

CHAPTER VI

THE BASIS IN AMUSEMENT

CHAPTER VI

THE BASIS IN AMUSEMENT

THE city industrial man of the lowest economic order, the intermittent worker for a bare subsistence
wage, is essentially primitive because he has few
and fluctuating motives to productive work. His estate
may be worse than that of his forbear of the solitudes,
for on the one hand, the bald dangers of death by cold,
hunger, and fear are minimized by a relief system which
will warm, feed, and soothe him; and on the other, his
immediate, well-adapted, and exciting contact with
nature has been destroyed by the town life to which his
organism painfully seeks adjustment. The tailor,
malplaced in one attitude all day, sewing other men's
coats that he may cover his own back, is not stirred by
the interest, the courage, the triumph, that thrill the
hunter when he tears off a bear's pelt for his winter
warmth. The baker in the hot darkness of the cellar
and the negro cook complaining to herself in wordless
gutturals over the kitchen stove make bread to satisfy
their hunger; but they work by indirection in an unnatural environment which rather checks than arouses
their bodily and mental activities. They are deprived
of that exciting approach to their desires from which in

former days such powerful emotions and instincts were evolved that they even now control. The rapid substitution of city phenomena for the nature processes in which the type developed is yet so new, so contrary to the physiology of the men who have to bear the severest abnormalities of city living, that their actions must be interpreted by the strong and persistent motives of past centuries.

The present necessity for tremendous adaptations to which biological functioning is hard pressed to respond, has the effect of weakening the appetites that characterize the older and more firmly established adjustments. Craving diminishes and the strength of motive wanes when the protesting organism is forced to adapt itself to bad air, poor light, fixed position, and routine occupation. Kindling, bracing hunger comes less often. Imagination, which developed and was in turn developed by a terrible and beautiful pantheism, becomes languid in the de-natured town. All that remains of this powerful motive to activity — the awe of physical phenomena and religious belief in magic — is a pleasant stirring of race memories while we watch legerdemain in amusement houses. Nature reactions are gone, and we have not replaced them; therefore, neither eye nor ear is the perfect instrument it was. One is dimmed and more listless; the other is jarred and unpurposed by the constant roar of city noises which have no message for the hearer. It is the frequent failure of correlation between a man's powers and his opportunities to exercise them which tempts him to find the excitement his nature craves by the artificial stimuli of vice. Rich ozone and the tang of winds once gave to the ancestors of the sedentary factory worker the zest in physical being for which immorality and intemperance are now mere counterfeits in the life of the city toiler. Drinking and the new sedative pleasures of smoking and saloon card-games are the vices of a faulty economic system, and an unintelligent attempt to enrich an impoverished, alien situation. They are irrational and extravagant, for they sate appetite and deaden acute pain without renewing force or directing vigor toward the day's work. How shall activity be made pleasurable again, and how shall society utilize the workingman's latent vitality in order to increase his industrial efficiency and give to him the rewards of energies, now ineffective, within his body and mind?

In order to emancipate him in the industrial world, it is necessary to educate him by methods radically different from systems that succeeded with men living in the country and working under the conditions of nature itself. These earlier educational theories depended upon the assumption that men beneath the dominion of nature could be made efficient by training their hands to overcome the savagery of land and water. Manual skill made the countryman safe just as it is the present guarantee of the high-grade city artisan whose able fingers earn $1000 a year. The town man, however, has overlaid and overwrapped nature with artifices; light, heat, and food come to him through mechanical media. In the country he lifted himself into apparently spontaneous and reciprocal relations with his material; in the town he still remains in automatic subordination to things. His perceptions are dull, his vision vague, and the machine he tends does not demand greater skill than he already possesses. He must enter civilization by some other route than that of a high differentiation of hand power applied to a simplified machine. Education must arouse him to the domination of his new world by stimulating eye and ear until he sees and hears fresh inducements to activity. It follows that he should be given a mobile body and mind in order that he may be made acquainted with the unimagined possibilities of his strange environment. The old cry, "Back to nature," must be translated into some slogan that will convey to city men a kindred meaning of variety, growth, imagination, and freedom of opportunity. The march of the lowly is not "back to nature interests," but "forward to communal interests."

THE BASIS IN AMUSEMENT

The basal producer cannot be adequately educated by arousing him to the value of the product of his own hands; but to interest him in the product of his group is to educate him to his full capacity. To teach him to do things in such a competent fashion that his faulty adjustment to nature becomes correct, is an ideal that must miss its goal when the pupil's environment is the factory. The returns from his own toil do not affect him as intimately as the product of the community's activity does; and therefore the educational emphasis should be laid upon his relation to the great entities of his city, instead of upon a little tool as it has been wielded by the isolated and primitive worker. He cannot be given enthusiasm for the spindles he guards or the broom with which he sweeps the streets, until he is stimulated by the communal life. It is the primary task of education to make him aware of that life, and to arouse him to participation in it through the common use of enormous units like the amusements and recreations of parks, theatres, " Coney Islands," department stores, settlements, free lectures, and socialized schoolhouses.

The education of the eye of such a man must precede that of his hand, for the hand without well-directed purposes cannot lift him from the static plane of a subsistence wage. The contrast between the gifts of the two forms of education is clear enough: that which carries the banner, "Back to nature," has given contact with things, inspired respect for the product of the hand, and developed love for the "fortress" kind of home. It teaches that beauty is in a mediæval craftsmanship and ugliness in the machine-made object, and turns the student toward Logic, History, and Literature. The other education that strives to incorporate men into urban civilization gives them contact with men and inculcates respect for civic efficiency and love for public works, schools, streets, and buildings. It points out where beauty exists in coöperative communal institutions, and fosters neighborhood pride and the spirit of association. Instead of restraining impulses and instincts, it seeks to free the imagination, to stir and spur the desires, and to concentrate pointless energies upon the coördination of man and city. The City Beautiful must precede the World Beautiful, and the poverty man must find his real home in the first. The rich man may go back to nature and buy a township or a mountain or a pine woods for the satisfaction of his sense of beauty, but the worker of an industrial age must learn how to possess the streets and to be proud or ashamed of them as the agriculturist is of his fields; he must look to the condition of the electric car as carefully as the farmer to his fences, and to his own recreational centres as the planter to his crops.

THE BASIS IN AMUSEMENT

The enjoyment of these vast contrivances may be offered as the immediate and visible returns of labor; the educator has only to reverse the accustomed order and place the æsthetic pleasures before the drill in moral restraints and the theory of saving. The love of life and not the fear of want should be the motive of activity in repressed peoples. Nor need the cost of education through the eye, if it is done on a large scale, be greater than that of a general system of manual training. The working-man would then be influenced as profoundly in his leisure as in the narrow routine of toil, and there would be at least a balance of power between eight hours of work and eight of rest. Each day ought to be complete in itself, for the marginal workers are not influenced by ideals of next year's capitalization. Pleasure should exist in to-day's eight hours of leisure, and round the cycle to satisfaction when the man enters the third period of sleep. He will wish then to repeat that day, to live it in fulness again and again, and in the slow expansion of its gratifications he will find new incentives to the work that provides them. The first rapid advance has been made when the desires have been intensified and multiplied until men who are now content to live five days on the earnings of two can no longer make both ends meet.

If they have few wants and less imagination, they may

never improve, for the organization of charity has tempered the raw need of clothing, shelter, and food until it is not insistent enough to overcome the marginal worker's inherent inclination to escape the monotony of sustained and systematic work; his lack of the primary necessities energizes him, at best, until he is for the moment fed and sheltered. Then he "lays off" — this odd-jobber who elects a lazy leisure as the greatest satisfaction. A negro family raising cotton in an Oklahoma village was recently lifted by an unprecedented surplus of $17 on their crop to a plane of slothful ease. The wife, who had been the peripatetic washerwoman of the town, refused to serve it; she declared that she had "nothing to work for." The husband deposited the $17 in the bank, asserting that he did not know what to do with it or with himself, since the rent was paid and the larder stocked. They are "very decent," the neighbors say; the community can find no fault with them as citizens. Yet they are a loss to society, because the economic frailties of primitive men are theirs, and because no way has yet been found to enlist such well-intentioned stragglers of industry — the guerillas of the subsistence line — into the steady ranks of disciplined producers.

It will be exceedingly difficult to incorporate them without preparing the way to the familiar and accustomed moral age by using all forms of recreation. On the first plane of development, men watch others do what they would like to do themselves; on the second, they exhaust their surplus energy in play; and in the third, they reflect on the consequences of facts and events. But as soon as social reformers and educators undertake to realize this concept with the fragmentary and confused means at their disposal, they encounter the opposing ideal of restraint, denial, and negation, which is half instinctively thrust forward by that large class of people who are either offended by the "bad taste" or the "low morals" of amusement which has not the imprint of their own more discriminating culture.

They believe it universally discordant because it jars upon their evolved refinements. "How successful that Greek art lecture was!" exclaimed the leader of an Irish boys settlement club. "I had it given twice because the boys misbehaved the first time. But I told them if they did it again I should never arrange another entertainment for them, and they really listened pretty patiently. They are a restless group at best." It is not beyond our wit to see why this policed and threatened club shuffled and whistled, or why the boys' faces lacked the expression of concentration and rapt anticipation of the circles about the Punch and Judy booth and the organ grinder with his monkey. If you take away the booth, you can no more recompense that audience than you could repay childhood should you ban the publication of Mother Goose, or placate the Irish boys to whom was given the free art lecture in place of the circus, to which they had voted their club funds.

Punch and the Clown are as valuable as the tragic and comic muses of the Greek drama, because they also mark an epoch in man's growth. The primitive man, de-energized by work, craves no more activity and is happy while he rests if he can be made to feel intensely. It is necessary, therefore, not only to start the current of his thought, but to direct it by the nearest and most direct stimulus. This exists in its most accessible form in the people's theatre, which utilizes material gathered from immemorial sources and sets forth the life process in the popular melodrama of the hour. The sweep of the imagination in the theatre is stronger than the contemplative love of nature in this type of man, and he is educated through the pleasurable outgo of varied emotions. The elemental action of the stage settles the succession of ideas and quickens thought in its deep, accustomed channels. We crave such memory-food, and know positive joy when it is served again and yet again. It is less a weakness to be "stage-struck" than an evidence of dawning idealism in barren, narrow lives. If we can find a natural expression for the longing after more experience, the starved individuality will unfold into the hero-worship age without jar or fret.

Melodrama is especially the agent of expression in American cities, where a heterogeneous population has forcibly broken with its traditions. To save our foreigners to society, the old things must not be destroyed; they must be harmoniously mingled with the new; many of the emigrant's traditions are as valuable as our own, and if we are skilful enough to preserve them in our lore the gain will be no less theirs than ours. Traditions are strengthened by commingling, and after each infusion the ideal takes a higher, purer form. Poetry, fiction, and the drama become more vigorous, more catholic, and more classic; and a great human uplift follows successful race assimilation, which is brought about by a blending of ancient race memories with individual experiences in the new environment. The man flagging at monotonous, exhausting toil gropes for equilibrium among the opposing influences of instinct, habit, imitation, and new conditions: yet each struggling force has potency and ought to find free outlet through the channels of amusement. Society might well develop an institution which shall become the vehicle of recreation as the home has become the vehicle of family life.

We have, however, gone no further than to permit men to exploit for private gain the craving to be amused. The workman is drawn hither and thither by the uncorrelated motley devices of selfish promoters and is often solicited by them until he has dissipated his vigor and lowered his moral tone. The deterioration which social workers note in the frequenters of dance halls follows the abortive attempt of the young toilers to find in varied movement the physical alterative of factory work. But the truth that dancing is both remedial and social is proved in the agencies controlled by settlements and clubs, where air, cleanliness, and space give the seeker the physical freedom he craves.

The emotional corrective of the barren industrial grind, at present, lies in the melodramatic and exciting presentation of life processes in the people's theatres, the cheap variety houses, and the concert halls. There once again the primitive man faces the conditions of the primitive world; the strong stimulus of the enemy who follows to the death, the awakened wit which casts about to baffle the cunning of the rival; the renewed imagining of hate, love, terror, curiosity, danger, daring, and fury — all the elemental stuff — concentrates the thoughts and momentarily rouses mental forces to a

keener effectiveness than any scheme of night schools
has yet discovered. The absorbing tumult swells
with sudden gusto the flattened chests of the beholders
and converts the audience into a purposeful, attentive
body of men. The cheap magician of a vaudeville
can excite the primitive curiosity of the mass and his
claptrap thrill it into thought. A shabby young man
recently listened with a rather scornful, roving air to a
vaudeville artist's assumption of invincible magnetic
powers. He scoffed audibly while "a committee from
the audience" came forward to accept a challenge to
lift the performer from the floor. When it appeared
unable to do so he settled to keen watching; as the trick
proceeded, his hands grasped more tightly the back of
the seat ahead, while his mind, aroused from inertia by
the magic recall of the past, gripped the problem.
He shook his head when the affair at length became in-
explicable and turned with an alert, pleased fright to the
stranger beside him. "Well," he said delightedly, "it
was sure the spirit world done that." The utility of
the hour was not destroyed because the trick was in-
soluble in his typically simple process of thought; the
worth of it lies in the quickened energy which radi-
ates from the shabby, beaming fellow, and is diri-
gible into productive fields. In a low-price theatre
an excellent melodrama sets free that intense emotion

which is the fulcrum for uplift. One of a party which saw "The Two Orphans" in Philadelphia was a young factory girl, who eagerly explained the scenes about to be presented. "I've seen it seven times — once every winter," she whispered; "and I certainly do enjoy looking forward to it. It's so good I have to cry." Her cheeks were red, her eyes liquid with the "fun" of tears and the sting of the primal passions. In this play the heroine is fruitlessly sought by the hero, who would wrench her from the bad old woman. Near the end a particularly aggravating escape is made, and the poor girl is thrust into the garret at the instant the hero bursts from the wings. "Where is she?" he cries, "I cannot find her!" This was too much for a fellow-hero in the audience, who half rose from his seat to shout, "For Gawd's sake, look upstairs!"

The desire to do, to be, to strive in our own persons, which is aroused by the sight of pleasurable activity in others, is appreciable by more advanced groups because it still flickers within themselves. We experience a bodily refreshment, a brightening of blood and tissue, as we watch the suppleness of a dancer, the posturing of acrobats, and the beautiful delicacies of wire walkers. We are attracted by danger, and the unguarded trapeze yields us a pleasant qualm. We enjoy the mock perils of the scenic railway and the real risks of the popular "loops" and "chutes," and say that they have given us "new" sensations, that are, in fact, as old as society itself. It is terror, grown delicious with the passage of time, that leads the child to the back of the widest jawed lion of the merry-go-round and makes him quiver when the beast begins to stir. Children and the more alert basal workers are deeply influenced by the experiences they acquire through their own bodily activity. Their physical functioning arouses emotion and keeps the interests active through the epoch of sports and play and up to the period when they cease to be briefly controlled by the impressions of eye and ear or by physical amusements. It is only the highest types of men who can mould their conduct by abstract thought and pure reflection; the lower must watch the instructive, enlightening deed itself and deduct right and wrong from vivid, simple pictures. This distinction operating in the workingman's world accounts for the differing effects there of the melodrama and the "yellow" press. The printed page is only partially pictorial; it has no integral part in our remote heredity; neither is it the exponent of the primitive man's history even when it deals with the primitive conduct, because it cannot represent with the naturalness which is logic the motives of action vividly enough for all the senses to perceive them. There may even be a distinct loss to the

[135]

unlettered mind while it attempts to translate the unfamiliar symbols that describe a local murder. Morbidity of thought, as imitative crimes have proven, sometimes follows the inartistic piecemeal representations of the printed page that lack (and here is the test) the supreme art which alone can call forth men's activity through unaccustomed channels. On the other hand, the stage tragedy, unfolded by living beings, must give the sequences and motives in such orderly development that sane dynamic impulses are aroused in the man who would not wish to know of an actual murder or who might read of it with unwholesome zest.

So while the unseen is of scant interest to society's raw recruit, the direct stimuli of his sense perceptions thrust him into voluntary exertions. To incorporate these objects which he can see and feel into the industrial world is to fix the spurs that prick to work. A circus, a national holiday, a camp meeting, arouse country people sharply and suddenly to a need of ready money. Coney Island attracts the city man as soon as he has achieved a bare subsistence. These primitive satisfactions pay their own way because the authority vested in them by distant ages is recognized by the half-dormant worker. The people's theatres wield that authority so potently that if they were managed by educators and philanthropists for purely social ends they too could pay their way on a schedule of prices within the reach of low-paid laborers. During a phase of many young workers' lives they regularly attend the theatre, engaging "season seats" in cheap houses for thirty or fifty cents a performance. Their zest for amusement urges them to submit to the discipline of work, and the habits formed for the sake of gratifying their tastes make the regular life necessary in industry easier and more pleasant. The boy who wishes to hold a steady job must learn to be punctual and responsible. If he retorts to his foreman and loses his place because of impulsiveness, he ultimately finds self-control and the patience of the long view. Honesty, application, adaptability through much pain, become his assests in his new bond with society. He recognizes the market value of cleanliness, for those who hire lay such emphasis upon it that the army which cleans cars, streets, and buildings must learn to see and to hate dirt. Physical neatness — a perception of personal dignity and worth — is thrust upon the man who is willing to work in the markets, stores, and hotels, or as manual helper in uniformed public service. A constant coercive power is exerted by the employer and the public while the primitive man is being introduced by his own augmenting wants into a regulated industrial life.

But as time passes, the habits formed for purely

selfish, economic needs become new motives in the improving type of man. The pleasure in the personal and environmental tidiness at first imposed upon him becomes an innate love of order for its own sake. The advantages of coöperation found in experience begin to move the primitive individualist. Industrial efficiency, fortified by the sense of enlarging relationships, brings the class to a plane where family life is desired and possible. The horizon of wants and consumption widens. The satiety of primitive desires which follows increased income, urges men to displace crude individual gratifications with grouped pleasures. It is as if they began to perceive social relationships which, like that long since established between bread and butter, give more pleasure together than could be obtained from the two taken singly. Such readjustments of values yielding an enlarged output of satisfaction from given quantities of material are the dawning of art and simple harmony which stir emotions to fresh intensity; and art will act henceforth as a motive to activity. But it is not a new motive — it is a primitive impulse made available for the progress of the city-industrial man. Decoration of one's self, one's dependants, and one's habitation follows the birth of self-consciousness, and ceremonials celebrated with music and masses of color are activities native to the aboriginal man; but the stored force of them cannot be utilized in the city man while he is stumbling at the perilous edge of dependence. Cleanliness ceases to be the more or less onerous requirement and becomes a widening æsthetic joy in the scrubbed floors of the worker's own house, the shining windows, the ebony stove, and in his well-washed children about a white-clothed table. The woman who in girlhood learned to be punctual at her factory bench impresses her acquired quality upon her family and is proud to be named by her tenement neighbors the most particular woman in the house. Thrilling with pride in the appearance of people for whom she is responsible and in objects which she possesses, she has a delight — new to her class — in precision, in simplicity of form, and in order. Her desire is to add to the number of her things, and because of the rapid cheapening of commodities this primary æsthetic longing is among the first to be gratified. The working-man's home is crowded with tawdry, unmeaning, and useless objects; each pointless ornament is loved, however, as the mark of superiority and success, and its enjoyment energizes the possessor.

It is at this point in education that most art teaching for the "masses" fails. The canons of advanced art have sprung from critical æsthetics and are not within the comprehension of the simple minds of those who find beauty and stimulus in mere ownership. Perceptions of technique, the selective faculty asserting itself through color, harmony, or historical sequence, instead of through simple utility and emotion — why should these difficult tests be laid upon the tenement? Rather let the first of all art forms — the æsthetics of addition — be supplemented and not reduced. The elaborated, unsanitary feather-beds which fill too much space in the Italian tenements, with their ornamental bolsters, pillows, and fringed bedding; the heavily embroidered gingham aprons which touch the broken shoes and frayed skirts of the women have positive values for their owners. It is a waste of energy to point out to the glowing purchaser the incongruity between her flowered and fragile dishes and the dingy oil-cloth of her kitchen table, as long as the conjunction expresses the hospitality which has become one of the greatest pleasures of her life. She is now the responsible housewife, and her house must mirror forth her virtues.

The home, church, school, city, and country in turn are idealized as centres of special groups of pleasures. The holiday, the festival, and the day of birth and marriage are decked with associations that raise the value of these group enjoyments far above the satisfactions of the mere goods consumed. Men lose interest in the more individual features of their lives and turn eagerly to those that are social. There is satisfaction in doing good work; industrial honor emerges, and the germ of civic goodness takes root. Pride in accomplishment culminates in an appreciation and a development of character; to be known as a well-cared-for husband, a generous father, and a contributor to fraternal organizations are aspirations which voice themselves as related values.

In the course of consumption expanding by orderly processes the new wants become complex, oppose each other, project themselves into the future, and demand forethought in their balances. The possibility of choice arises, and the option upon to-day's pleasure is measured beside that of next year. The worker steadily and cheerfully chooses the deprivations of this week in order to secure the gratifications of a coming holiday. From this motive the virtue, abstinence, at length emerges and is established as a motive for activity. Men idealize the future and depreciate the present; they advance into a period of restraint and morality, puritan in essence but various in form. Their investment in to-morrow's goods enables society to increase its output and to broaden its productive areas. It is capitalization, the subjective side of which is so intense a vision of the future that man is able to see family or country waxing in power down the generations, and to experience a religion which reconciles him to the pains of life by promises of pleasures after death.

The higher or conventional moral epoch is reached after primitive desires have been utilized under industrial conditions, and new values have been created by a concordant grouping of the objects in the environment. Here is the time of restraints and not of expansions. Primitive desires are partially suppressed; there is a more careful consumption of goods and the familiar practice of morality subordinates the present to the past and the future. All this might be uneconomic and a restraint on work but for the fact that it encourages the growth of capital. Saving is the economic side of morality. Morality and economic motives are reconciled in the degree that restraints on work are idealized and made an integral part of morality. Sunday observance was idealized long ago, and to-day other prohibitions are being transformed into moral imperatives. Morality without the spirit of work may degenerate, but with that spirit Consumption is grouped around fresh centres and the evils of the primitive world with its overestimation of the present are avoided.

The world-movement which shall uplift all classes must be along the line of least resistance. Vice must first be fought by welfare, not by restraint; and society is not safe until to-day's pleasures are stronger than its temptations. Men must enjoy, and emphasis should be laid again upon amusement so extended and thorough that primitive people may be incorporated by its manifold activities into the industrial world. It is a vital link connecting the primitive with the advanced eras, where work has ceased to be wholly painful, irksome, and tedious, because its returns are immediate and vivid. Amusement is stronger than vice and can stifle the lust of it. It is a base of economic efficiency upon which depends the progress of multitudes. When men and women have withstood the allurements of vice and learned work-habits, then the steps beyond are fairly well-paved. The church and the home can moralize and induce character, the school can clarify purpose, and the settlement can socialize the material ready in the industrial world.

CHAPTER VII

THE BASIS IN CHARACTER

CHAPTER VII

THE BASIS IN CHARACTER

THE relations between men and nature reach their final expression in systems of ethics and codes of conduct. The two great formative forces, religion and education, have trained us for future salvation and present usefulness by the discipline of pain, and both have inflicted it by artifice when the disciple's lot was too smooth to prepare him for life's troubled way. Men applaud the scars upon their fellows and smile indulgently at the thorn in the sole of the barefoot boy, thinking placidly that he will travel farther because it has plagued him there. They ardently seek to frame within themselves a satisfying philosophy the antithesis of their desires and denials, endeavors and disasters, toil and emptiness, goodness and calamities; and they have built a structure, which, if it does not satisfy, at least has reconciled them to the "sweet uses of adversity"; and now society believes without reflection that the finest character is the product of suffering. Teachers for a long time believed that education was the enforcement of difficult tasks and that playtime was a concession to natural weakness, that might be ignored as a mere pause between the valuable prosecutions of uninviting tasks. They have feared that the work toward which students showed a decided inclination was a pitfall of ease and sloth; it would become a lax world, thought the conservative instructor, if the young were permitted to follow the line of least resistance, which is that of the greatest interest. Work that was a pleasurable activity was sacrificed during the plastic years to a mechanical discipline that often failed because the educator did not comprehend the origin and limitation of the philosophy of development through pain. Character is made by obstacles, the moralists say; and the greater the obstacles the better the man. To do is to suffer; there was no room in the old world of deficit which scars our memories for another maxim — to be, is to do pleasurable work. So it has come about that the character of the martyr is revered and he becomes an epic figure in church and state, a hero who has been able to convert his portion of the universal misery and his sentence of defeat into a beautiful surrender.

The person who is able to suffer nobly or to dominate his fellows magnificently is so admirable and so worthy of emulation that we finally believe the conditions which made him are of themselves mysteriously right. James Martineau bids us remember, when hard pressed by the misery of life, that "a world without a contingency or an agony could have had no hero and no saint." Montaigne admonishes us that the very name of virtue presupposes difficulty, and adds that virtue cannot be exercised unless there is a battle. It were better, then, that society should continue to suffer than that it should lose the spectacle of the sufferers who have made an art of wretchedness. To attain to their perfection we embrace the means, and voluntarily surround ourselves with obsolete discomforts for the cure of our souls. We fête and saint the ascetics who elect the life of hunger, cold, and isolation, and, although we may live in a land of warmth and plenty, contemplate with humble aspiration the exemplar of their careers. We are hero-worshippers, constantly looking for the man who can lead us past our dangers and guide us in crises that hazard our lives, and when he has come we dote on his qualities and use him as our ideal. His apotheosis does not long depend upon the timeliness of his rescue, for he looms a waxing heroic figure after his death, and under different circumstances. Virtue clings to him after another order has been established, necessitating other rescuers. The soldier as Hero is not discarded by a peace society until new troubles have brought forth a new protector to replace him. The city boy will admire the brave fireman as long as men live in inflammable houses; yet the good result of the dashing spectacle of professional valor upon the character of the boy is not an argument against the advantages of a fire-proof city. A city "without a contingency or an agony" could well dispense with the heroes of casualty departments and the saints of the hospital wards. The sacrifices implacably demanded and gloriously paid to religion and to patriotism are the sources of the great epics, but one would not continue the wars of faith and of race in order to perpetuate the glorious hierarchy of martyrs in a majestic song.

Men are now squarely confronted with two issues. They may continue to cultivate ancestral qualities of strife and sacrifice in surroundings of peace and plenty, or they may consciously develop a new type of man fitted for the society without poverty toward which we aspire. If human beings were trees we would plant them in the sheltered valleys, where food is ready at their roots. No culturists would choose a mountain top for an arboretum or instil beauty by breeding plants at the edge of the frost line. They grow less well there, although their wild and painful outlines may give the artist a story of noble battle. The farmer who tries to improve his stock does not select hardships, as men do in breeding character. The sheep and cattle are given easy opulent pastures; a tough and bony ranger of the prairies cannot remain the hero of the fenced ground and heated barns. The market steer weighs much more than it did before the western cattle raiser had mitigated climate and warded enemies from his stock. Cold and starvation are now negligible quantities in the great ranches, and the breeds that were notable for ability to withstand them give way to varieties that may be adapted to neither emergency. Leadership has gone from the animal whose triumph is mere survival and comes to the creature whose vitality is stored as a surplus fund for productive, socialized uses. The value of the domesticated animal depends less upon tendon and toughness; mechanical aids, like fences and shelters, replace cartilage in the vital economy and enable sheep and beeves to be revalued according to strength convertible into their share of the social surplus — milk, wool, or leather. A lamb wins a prize if its fleece is long and heavy enough to imperil its escape from the wolf that no longer exists, but whose ancestors may have eaten the forbears of the lamb. The virtue of the animal follows its uses in the present and is measured not by its ability in the past, but solely by its promised capacity in a man-made and softened future. Its vitality — which can become surplus only as the body is protected from primitive rigors — is directed to productive channels as a man's vitality may be when he, too, need not fully expend his energy in self-protection.

But the virtue and morality of the man is believed to depend upon his power to embrace dangers and to smile resignedly upon suffering; and herein the educator, reversing the course of natural science and blind to its illustrations, depletes the social values of the student in an attempt to save him from archaic dangers by applying the lad's reserves to individual and uncalled-for resistance to suffering.   A follower of Rousseau recently excited the anger of a policeman who threatened to arrest him for cruelty to his children unless he should clothe more warmly the two tearful little boys shivering in the winter blasts.   The father expounded that he was hardening them.   "What for?" rejoined the officer.   "Haven't you a furnace, and aren't the schools warm, and aren't they making an ordinance to heat street cars?   Nobody will make them cry but yourself.   Those children ought to have long stockings on."   The policeman perceived that the boys were not being educated for the world in which they were to live; he was reasoning toward the future and men's rights in it, and knowing little of the dangers we escaped before the days of universal heating plants, was annoyed by the father's apparent irrationality of method.   He would have none of a society in which children must cry in order to become strong, good men.   There was better work for those reluctant legs to do on the bleak day when they trotted back and forth within reach of the warmth now more natural to cities than tempestuous nature is. The policeman could have directed the father to agencies that would have enlisted the shivering muscles in joyful, comprehended toil promptly recompensed and therefore enlisting fresh and happy workers.

The ennobling quality of sacrifice is in the agonizing surrender of the soul, in the melancholy glory of pain borne with a purpose, and in the forlorn attempt to undo evil. The methods, like all methods of the weak, are circuitous and wasteful, and succeed only in arresting the forces of decay without being able to plant the germs of progress. Sacrifice is an abortive deed conceived in deficit and arrested action. In the realm of character and of conduct it is an acquired pessimism teaching that we exist in an evil medium and must not value the life we have in it. Detach yourself from the world, divide yourself from your fellows, cry the frightened moralists, for thus you will find an easy severance from life and avoid its incalculable pains. In a society, however, which is conscious of ample resources and is learning that coöperation can abolish poverty by saving men instead of spending them, the philosophy of the disciplinary values of hardship rings false. The opulence and triumphs of powerful young nations like

America make hearts recoil from the barren energies of misery. The thought of suffering, which was
calmly contemplative under mediæval Christianity,
has now the sting of sharp impatience in it, and the
very capacity of endurance is diminished. Russian
fiction is so packed with immobile misery that un-
relieved reading of it sickens the sensitive American.
The realism of the picture sears the fancy, and lacerates
the pliant, mobile minds of happier races. Such art
scarifies, and its moral value for the non-Russian lies in
its renewal of common bonds through a common past,
and the results of that brotherhood in gifts of money and
an asylum. The morality of sacrifice is the antithesis
of the morality of progress, and the two types contrast
each other with increasing emphasis. The morality of
inaction, unlike that of expanding activities in a fear-
free society, is not an absolute principle or a permanent
ideal, for its validity is limited to primitive conditions
and it becomes valueless when its purpose can be ful-
filled by a readjustment of nature. At bottom sacrifice
is a physical and animal trait which has come to us in
the course of biological development; and when lifted
to a foremost place on the spiritual plane, it at length
saps energy because it wrests away the fruits of action,
and by pouring vitality into negation and undoing, keeps
the world a poorer place than it might be.

THE BASIS IN CHARACTER

The improvement of nations is measured by that margin of riches and of power left from the cost of living; and that character is greatest in the new society which is trained to give its excess to immediate ends; and that course becomes normal and therefore moral which enables individuals to add to the superabundance of the general goods. Generosity is the moral vehicle of their distribution, and the building of the social surplus demands an increasing use of it. Generosity has little in common with sacrifice though both spring from the same instinct, for it is freed completely from personal anguish and foreboding. Modern trained generosity and primary instinctive sacrifice are at the opposite poles of the imagination; the one being the fruit of security and the other of danger. In the beginning, however, the imagination was directed by fear: the deer imagines danger behind each unknown noise and the man an enemy in a waving bush. From all-pervading terror men passed into the narrowing grip of superstition which is imagination under the dominion of fear. Imagination, functioning through superstition, does restrain, but it also narrows and debases people living in unfriendly conditions and causes them to be governed by a fantastic code made from their terrified fancies. In such case we need only to prepare a broader base, by uprooting the last of the superstitions and setting the imagination at work upon the wide interests in accordance with its natural tendency in people of large surplus vitality. In a rich environment where energy is stored men become idealistic, artistic, and moral. The surplus energy of the well-paid laborer points out to him new objects of desire, and if they seem attainable, enthusiasm is generated within the man to carry him thither. Enthusiasm is born of energy and varied desires. When it broadens, deepens, and finds everywhere new centres, its objects become ideals of goodness, of patriotism, of culture, and of art. It is the transformation of interests into morality, opposing itself to the counter-transformation in the imagination of objects of pain into superstitions. The plasm of to-morrow's world is activity, and the life germ is work. Work, then, in a normal resourceful environment is the concrete expression of surplus vitality flowing along interesting, productive, and recompensing processes, whose fruit and purpose in civilization is character. When imperfect civilization balks and distorts the free play of pleasurable activities, toil becomes a monstrous, incalculably evil thing; we call it drudgery and the man condemned to it reverts to a lower kind of creature, unpliant, crudely limited in passions, early matured, and prematurely decayed. Drudgery and hardship are one, for they are the method of arriving at ends by depletions without full and joyous renewals. The labor of children arrests them all too often at that stage of growth in which they are seized by Industry; the kind of work offered them during the reign of the machine forces them into abortive maturity and imperils character; we make them work without giving them love and pleasure in it. The beautiful and frail organism is strained too far to take firm shape in later years; monotonous toil which does not create objects of interest to the maker destroys the wholesome tissues of the life. And if it is so long continued that the mind ceases to trace cause and effect between labor and reward, it pours into society the tramp laborer and the petty criminal. It does violence to the normal budding character of youth — to flexibility, plasticity, and vivid interest in processes rather than in results. In adolescence activity should find exit in the experimental plays of which manual training and civic training, books and organized recreation, are component parts. In such natural simplicity of conduct is the matrix of character which is valueless to the exploiter, but which is the source of social income that should not be touched until slow, natural coördinations have been completed. To suppress the natural traits and force forward those acquired in industry, anticipates by artifice the cautious unfolding of characters, prematurely ripens the man, and casts upon society the dead weight of a class too old to work at forty, and too undeveloped to join the wise counsels of the elder mentors of the nation.

The economic virtues as they have sprung up in certain happy places are the harvests of work done in harmony with the nature of men and of leisure which is the culmination of labor. For toil without purposeful and occupied leisure is unfilled purpose, a process arrested midway. If the working epoch develops the eye, the hand, and the brain to efficiency, leisure develops the judgment, and by stimulating variety in the consumption of goods relieves the inevitable monotony of work in the machine age. At this moment of social evolution one might indeed say that while the economic virtues are the product of work, the whole character is formed in leisure — its other half — because the motives of the ideal society are there rather than in machine labor.

The farm labor of America, with its variety, its alternation of exertion and rest, its distinctive merrymakings and its obvious, direct rewards, has been a treasury whence we draw some of the national aptitudes that bring success in urban occupations. Adaptability is a work virtue that paves the way to economic initiative; prudence balances the decisions of men who must forecast the thunder-storm threatening the grain; both weave themselves into the durable texture of the mind and are rather obscured than torn away even when they appear to have been destroyed. The seeds of virtues and of vices are within a man; he may become competent and well-to-do under one situation, or an underfed laborer driving himself half drunk to his hateful task under another. Hope and fear alternate violently when he is near the margin of subsistence. When fear is there, hope is apparently dead; yet hope is a permanent quality in the poor, and vanquishes fear on a good day. Observers who have never experienced want say the poor lack balance; but they live in an unbalanced world where they are bent to and fro by the strong play of emotions which are directly governed by a bad season, or one of gross surfeit; of peace or war; cold or heat; the joyous religious worship of spring, or the cringing abasement before storm demons; and by utter victory or absolute defeat in war. At the margin of the world there is not room or time for many emotions, nicely adjusted and slowly affecting men. There are a few which possess them suddenly and then recede before new conditions and its appropriate primitive passion. The evolution of character in young races is marked by repression and release; it is an affair of contrasted states of being, and finds its analogue already worked out in botany where the active and

[159]

dormant characters of plants are described as existing simultaneously in a species even when one group of qualities appears to have been routed. The environment determines the result of the struggle, and so it does in the social characters of men. The peace situation that routs fear and establishes confidence is followed by a series of progressions which develop the poverty man as naturally as some hidden influence stamps one of several possible ancestral colors upon a plant. When favorable surroundings and the work virtues have suppressed the crudest fears, a second and superior quality, the initial or parental form of which has been implanted in past eras of comparative plenty, reappears to function strongly in the improved conditions. The higher derived types are the social virtues sprung from seed long since planted in the animal and savage worlds, and remaining latent until a rich industrial era makes them potent. Here are sympathy, generosity, justice, courage, honor, and their equals, in place of the social vices that rage in bad times. Envy, cunning, and revenge reappear in evil times; the greedy child is not to be wondered at as an unaccountable disgrace to his nursery training since he is only a naïve reminder that men once had to gorge themselves. Cunning is an evidence of the old struggles; it is an animal quality belonging to creatures that would fail in direct conflict, and its alternate is courage that springs from good conditions. The social virtues are the consequents of bonds formed when men entered group relationships, and occupy, as it were, a plane midway between the economic and the ultimate moral virtues typified by abstinence, fortitude, chastity, and thrift.

In our own experiences we observe the rise of economic, social, or moral characteristics which must have lain dormant in our neighbors during the control of their alternates, so swiftly do they advance to action and so maturely do they fulfil themselves therein. The power of work upon character is illustrated by the story of a milliner's errand girl. Her family history is that of illiterate and parasitical people, intermittent and unenthusiastic workers with few of the economic virtues and many lively memories of industrial vagabondage. This daughter shirked and blundered along in a hazy indifference until a friend suggested to her the idea of a normal school training and a teacher's career. After two years of blind effort she seemed to bring from some hidden treasury an assortment of qualities that have carried her nearly to the close of her chosen journey, over a road difficult to the verge of impassability and seldom offering a breathing place of rest and cheer. She became cleanly, cheerful, equable, and punctual. Self-control, thrift, and perseverance emphasized themselves in her conduct. Vivid interests and responsive virtues overcame the economic and social vices which child labor had fostered within her. With less than the average mental capacity, without charm of mind or person, she is succeeding by the force of character freed within her by the touch of circumstance. The true method of character building was found for this handicapped worker by her own discovery of mastering desire, and through a philosophy which spurs men to the goal of a higher wage where sacrifice, deprivation, and renunciation become diminishing requirements of survival.

This illustration is not used because it is new, but because it is typical. In every community one may find cogent examples of the outburst of sudden forces that uplift individuals and prove that character building is not an organic process, but a regeneration of latent powers transferring the supremacy from one group of ideas to another. A natural evolution effects changes less rapidly than regeneration does. The weak latently possess the powers that the strong display; and the sudden transformation of the weak into the strong, which we see daily, reveals the inherent qualities of human nature. In this regeneration — this new birth without the shackles of ancestral shortcomings and past misfortunes — the imagination is the dominant power; but it acts as a vivifying force only on those who have a fund of surplus energy. The weak and exploited never can release themselves from the drudgery of the moment. Their imagination functions on the pains they bear and holds them by the superstitions it breeds. But efficient work yields them a surplus which going out as a mental force turns the imagination upon pleasurable events and ideas instead of upon those that are sources of pain and fear. Such is the sudden transformation that seems like a new creation. Fleeting fancies are subordinated to enduring desires and are finally suppressed when the two conflict. Interest is thus transferred from the monotony and disappointments of the moment to the complete day, holding work, amusement and rest; and from the complete day, with its round of duties and pleasures, the interest is again extended to the complete life of permanent social relations. A complete day with all its parts clearly related subjects the impulses to control, and a complete life fully visualized directs the outgo of energy and makes it effective. The great ends of life thus become dominant, shape the daily routine, and repress pleasures and impulses which are out of harmony with the long view. It is this change that evokes character. Character is aroused by vivid ideas and long-sought ends. It is never built out of new material or improved by hardship and restraint.

It often happens that the simplest means attain the greatest ends. Taken alone, pleasure appears sinful, and work is a drudgery, but when the two are united in just proportions the effects seem magical. The activity of a man moving about in a world sufficiently safe to let him do earnestly what he wants to do will groove itself into goodness as the earlier activity ran into the groove of renunciation. Vice is energy aborted by the lack of variety, the imprisonment of desires, and the blunders of short-lived races. It is a miscarriage of vital force due to unnatural conditions and its manifestations are phases of the exploitation of creatures in fear. The bounds of action in an industrial society ought to be set by the experience of the individual in it, and not by the landmarks that safeguarded the earlier agriculturist; the restraint upon the action of either of them should be subject to the rules growing from a healthful environment, and determined by the economic virtues fostered in it. The code itself must be framed to arrest to-day's particular perils, and so save to-morrow from the grip of undemocratic privilege. Work — even the urban work of this industrial epoch — may place men in friendly, joyous relations with nature, and strengthen character without the cost of pain.

CHAPTER VIII

THE BASIS IN SOCIAL CONTROL

CHAPTER VIII

THE BASIS IN SOCIAL CONTROL

VIVID interests, energy, and awakened natural ability are the elements that give character to men. A man of character is one whose inner self finds complete expression through his activities, and such an one breaks the fetters of tradition and of place, effecting changes by which he profits and which stimulate other men in new ways. He is the man who is economically free, the self-emancipated, sometimes called the self-made man, to distinguish him from the classified orthodox follower of circumstance. If he produces brilliant results, we call him a man of genius. Yet the elements in him are inherent in others and would exhibit themselves in their action if they possessed surplus energy and were in direct contact with nature. The aggressive man is the natural man, and not he who is depleted and obedient. Those who discard tradition, following their nearest interests, and by their special powers of endurance and courage dominating their fellows, are merely men who have the qualities without the restraints of their neighbors. If all men were given energy and opportunity, they would forge ahead as self-made men do, and like them would break routine and tradition. The freedom and energy that spell progress are destructive of social discipline, and a decline in morality seems always to follow the self-assertion of success. But this view is only partial, for many of the saving virtues are also natural and make effective bulwarks when they are developed by favoring circumstances. Sympathy, generosity, justice, and manliness are rooted deep in human nature. But it is equally true that the unsocial passions — yes, even the great vices — are firmly based in a long-standing heredity. Human nature has antagonistic elements, and the natural man is buffeted about and often destroyed by opposing forces springing from his inner self. They are born with him, live in him, and die only to spring up afresh in his children. Virtue is real; but so is sin. To strengthen the one and to weaken the other is the source of all progress outside of a primitive world where the crude processes of nature themselves whip men into shape. But while vices and virtues are hereditary, morality itself is a restraint modifying human nature by eliminating existing qualities or by adding something new to character. Morality is a complex of simpler qualities so arranged that the social elements in human nature control the unsocial. It is not a problem of elimination or of growth, but of control. "Social control," a happy phrase coined by Professor Ross, is used here not to include everything social, but to contrast social and non-social. The phrase, then, signifies restraint that makes action moral in distinction from the unrelated impulsive action governing the primitive world and the unsocial life of to-day. In this way the growth in natural characters, which is evolution, may be contrasted with the increase of control, which is morality. It is necessary to make the comparison explicit, because many thinkers affirm that progress is possible only through the evolution of character. They hold rigidly to the doctrine that progress is the elimination of the unfit and that only the slow processes of centuries can graft the new characters that will raise human nature to a moral plane. It is generally agreed that little or no evolution of this sort is now going on, and probably there has been none since society was divided at the dawn of history into distinct classes. Our heredity is primitive heredity, changed in no marked degree by the course of civilization. The social sentiments of modern nations are, moreover, opposed to elimination. We protect the weak instead of exposing them; we restrain the strong instead of giving them full power. We give to those who have not, and take from those who have. These general principles combined with the influences of class differentiation will surely check for generations, if not forever, the sharp elimination upon which animal evolution depends. But even if a development in character through contest should take place, and the strong characters be matched against the weak as animals meet each other in grim combat, it is not likely that the social qualities would survive when so pitted against the unsocial. From their very nature they are opposed to elimination and the suffering it entails. Sympathy must go out to succor the weak, charity must aid the poor, and justice the oppressed. Neighborliness and kind-heartedness thrive in the help that those in temporary distress give each other. Without these qualities we might have a superman with excellent adjustment to nature; but if this superman mocked the weak instead of saving them, his strength, excellence, and beauty would be those of an animal. He would have power but not virtue. Evolution in character may help our distant descendants — but our problem is of to-day, and we must solve it with the means at hand. Control alone can span the chasm which the conflicting elements in human nature make in moral life. And this social control acts, not by creating a new and dominant motive, nor by modifying human nature; it sets one part of it over against another, and gives weak characters power over those with more natural vigor.

THE BASIS IN SOCIAL CONTROL

It moves through traditions, beliefs, and ideals, and not through individual discipline, restraint, or limitation. It does not alter a man's psychology or his physique; it affects him by changing his relations to others. Men's activities are determined partly by their natural characters and partly by the social traditions they accept. Social control acts through the latter, and to understand it we must discover how traditions, beliefs, and ideals are generated, how they arouse dormant powers in men, and put stamina in motives that otherwise would be too weak to find expression.

It is easy to see that men are at times sympathetic and generous. The crude, strong passions are often sated, or great disasters may give the social spirit an extraordinary impulse. But conditions do not always favor social qualities any more than the sun shines every day. And then a strong counter-current brings the unsocial to the fore. It is not enough at such a time to account for sympathy or greed, for selfishness or generosity; the task is to find how one tendency becomes so firmly established that it dominates the other. Control causes the habitual ascendency of certain traits, and so orders the life that opposing tendencies seldom appear. Objective situation directs control in its first stage; in the second its source is psychic.

A frontier camp is the stock illustration of the first.

Men come together for a single purpose, such as the mining of gold, and with their common aim in full view it is possible to organize a government the general advantage of which is apparent to every member of the group. The bandit, the cheating gambler, and the thief are the exceptions, who, repudiating control, are driven out by vigilance committees. The New England town meeting is another instance in which interests coincide and a community unites to further common ends. A more conspicuous effect of objective situation is the Holy City or the Paradise of religious literature. The traveller crossing the desert, blinded by sun and sand, suddenly sees a fertile oasis with its walled city. It is no wonder that the rest and peace the sight foretells inspire the ecstatic thought that such a haven is the reward of the good at the end of life's journey.

But control reaches its full development, not in these simple situations, where the interests of all coincide, but in the complex relations to which they are extended, where interests diverge. Its psychic power lies in the subordination of interests to ideals. It is said that while ordinary men may extend the influence of ideals only a great man can give them birth. This is an error, for ideals are born of situations and are from the first clear and simple because their source is. Their very simplicity drives the new truth home even in the minds

[172]

of the dullest. The law of diminishing returns was discovered by the most stupid body in England — a committee of the House of Lords. English agriculture at the close of the Napoleonic wars was so abnormal that any one could see how the high price of food brought poor land into cultivation. A committee, even if it was stupid, could not but stumble on the pertinent facts that formulated the law. But their perception of it does not account for its subsequent vogue. The real question of control is, Why did a nation, naturally optimistic and in a period of rapid industrial advance, accept this hopeless doctrine and permit it to curb their thinking for generations? Why also do teachers in America, where notoriously it never has been in operation, hold devoutly to it and spend their time expounding a lame philosophy to their classes?

It is rather these aspects of control that have to be explained than the origin of the idea. Stupidity can see, if the atmosphere is clear, but why are the wise held in control by preconceived consequences of the vision? It is not difficult to understand how the thought of a protective tariff took form. Manufacturers always desire to exclude outside rivals from their home market. But the great mass of a nation wants cheap goods. Why have they permitted high prices, and why do they believe that their prosperity is due to this subordination of their interests? Where one man is consciously benefited by the tariff, there are ten who accept it because it is associated in their minds with national independence, economic freedom, a high standard of life, and the growth of capital. The minority dominate the majority because their national beliefs and ideals have become blended with the concept of tariff restrictions. When there is social control of this sort, the logic of tariff advocates is of little consequence. It is not their arguments, but the causes of control that need attention. It is also easy to find where the doctrine of a closed shop arises. A body of laborers can see how it is to their advantage to shut out competitors from their occupation. But how comes it that when a strike is called other groups of workmen will uphold them in the face of their own interests? And why do the unemployed, who would naturally seek work and gladly displace other men, ardently support the strikers? There are innumerable instances of this form of control which balks the individual and alters the development of whole nations.

It is often said that the cause of this divergence of interests and action is in habit and routine. After beliefs have been established, habit and routine do perpetuate them, but they cannot account for the spread of belief in new regions. Many of us observe Sunday as a mere habit, but why did the Puritans accept a belief imported from a distant land and originating under different circumstances from those in which they lived? We often think that beliefs of a restrictive sort are survivals dating from primitive times, when superstition and ignorance prevailed. But American constitutional precedents are the growth of the last century, and they limit political life as rigidly as dietary laws restrain the Hebrews. Social control is not an old decaying fact. It springs up from fresh roots in every age. New beliefs are rising and spreading to-day as vigorously as they ever have done. These beliefs originate in two ways. In one an impressive picture fixes the imagination, which then projects the local vision over larger areas, where it becomes a principle or an ideal. In the other it arises from a reasoned connection between causes and effects, which enables us to anticipate new pleasure upon the appearance of well-recognized causes of past joys. The generation of beliefs, either by imagination or by reason, coincides with strong interests, which in their development must serve as the outlet of the surplus energy. Routine and habit are sparing of energy and are resorted to by the physically or mentally depleted. But surplus energy stimulates the imagination and inspires the boldness and daring which invite people to disregard the old landmarks of pain and to seek the enjoyments that lie in new experiences and in untried regions. The physically strong break away from restraint, and the physically weak are cowed into subjection by the terrors of the unknown. Prosperous times and the great rewards of enterprise are the strongest incentives to new beliefs, because they intensify happiness, afford freer play to the imagination, and give new material for inductive reasoning. Shift the conditions from prosperity to adversity, introduce disease and famine, let war bear its harvest of suffering, or let the dangers and uncertainties of an occupation multiply, and a swarm of superstitions will appear to fasten men more firmly to the sources of their ills and to perpetuate their miseries long after the inciting causes have disappeared. Superstitions and bigotries are the remnants of the world's failures preserved by the routine and narrow habits of those who fail. It is easier to impress a superstition than to create a belief, since it demands no energy to refrain from doing, while it takes energy to test unknown paths. But when the satisfaction of desires has given surplus energy, enthusiasm and imagination are easily aroused and open the road to new beliefs. The upward steps that follow fresh energy are: interest in the new, desire for experience, and, finally, a flow of the imagination. A visualization of good fortune, or the realization of happiness, yields the zest that is necessary for the renewal and adaptation of belief. An attained advantage, a realized benefit, sustains each belief; and a suffered penalty, or an arresting threat, is beneath each superstition.

Control through harmonious interests and noble ideals tends to degenerate, because it is more easily maintained by rules and habits than by renewed energy and fresh experiences. We may define the elevation of experience into ideals as attractive social control, for the reason that men's interests and their quest of happiness lead them into it. The other kind ought to be named restrictive social control, for here habit and routine limit the activities and the fear of pain is a constant depressing force, holding men within fixed bounds. Restraint blurs men's sensibilities, narrows the imagination, and leaves the primitive passions master. There follows a steady descent to lower levels and a degeneration into primitive conditions.

Beliefs in their early forms are always attractive and uplifting. Christian Science furnishes a notable example of their efficacy. Its motive power is happiness, to which much is added by the determined exclusion of the idea of pain. The conduct imposed by such a system of attractive control ennobles character. Early Christianity possessed the redemptive, exalting quality,

N   [177]

with a completeness that revolutionized the character of a whole state; for the concept of a bodily resurrection gave hope and cheer to its followers crushed by the hopeless outlook of earlier faiths. The degeneration from the belief in life eternal to the fear of endless pain came later when the attractive aspects of Christianity had become the habits, traditions, and ceremonies of the present.

In the exercise of social control we observe one more manifestation of the principle of surplus and deficit. Restrictive control prevails in periods when saving is necessary; economy hampers intellectual growth so that ideals and institutions lapse into barren formulæ, traditional rule, and defiant superstitions. The static condition of natural characters brought on by perishing social evils need not arrest progress, and will not, if men are placed where they may have access to a surplus. Improve industrial conditions, enlarge income, and new forms of social control will draw men forward into civilization. A single age of control would do what epochs of natural evolution could not. Although the unsocial cannot be eliminated, it may be suppressed by bonds of control so closely but yet so carefully and intelligently drawn that men would scarcely become aware of their own weakness. And all this may be done with the aid of forces now in active operation. The philosophy of deficit, which has long colored men's thoughts, deeds, and institutions must give way to an enthusiasm that revolts from old opinions. Such an enthusiasm is more necessary than one directed merely against old conditions. Income makes capital, and capital is ever improving the environment. But opinions, creeds, and superstitions live on endlessly, unless overcome by resolute men ready to suffer martyrdom for new ideals. Income will change conditions, but opinions yield only to the public service of devoted and self-sacrificing men. The old sacrifice, idealized in the age of deficit, consisted in the giving up of material advantages. The mother gave her substance to her child, and the patriot his life for the state, and men were martyred to benefit posterity. This subordination of one man to another is no longer necessary. The growth of income-altruism remodels situations; and service-altruism builds a new environment of ideas and beliefs. Sacrifice is a well-established quality. It is only necessary to turn it in new directions to make it as useful in the transformation of public opinion as it formerly was in saving children or in feeding the hungry. Men may face a deficit and turn its hardships into a process of upbuilding. And so may they enjoy a surplus and sink into vice. The whole community cannot but be hardened and lowered by a persisting deficit. Neither can it long resist the buoyancy and zest for the new that follows prosperity. In the end the new ideas will prevail, and the fresh enthusiasm of their devotees will create an environment of idealism which will uplift and control a nation.

The social forces of a community flow in directions easily traced. The interests and desires of men urge them into situations that inculcate habits of industry. An adequate reward for labor will always summon forth the economic virtues and transform them into habits. The social virtues and also the social vices existed in the animal world and perhaps have not been modified for ages. They cannot be removed or radically altered except by a long-continued evolutionary process; they are, however, suppressed or released by circumstances. The control over them is restrictive or attractive in the degree that the fear of punishment or the hope of reward sways men. Old forms of control are usually restrictive, because they represent past beliefs so petrified by age that the connections between them and their origins are lost. But in new situations, and with the energy that a surplus gives to prosperous nations, men are led on to more general concepts and away from limitations of early antagonisms. Vigor and enthusiasm construct a higher ethics, the practice of which unites unlike races. Prosperity draws men into larger groups, which will ultimately melt into a denationalized fraternal humanity. Here is control that overcomes race, creed, and the natural differences of men; it is sustained by universal forces so attractive that it subdues vices and casts aside the crude traditions and punishments of our ancestors.

In the table that follows, the effects of control upon virtues and vices are contrasted with qualities that are inherited and those that are acquired under the pressure of the economic environment.

Economic Virtues	Social Virtues	Social Vices	Restrictive Control (Morality)	Attractive Control (Ethics)
Application / Adaptability	Pride / Honor	Selfishness / Greed	Chastity / Fortitude	World Peace / Unrestricted Commerce / Brotherhood of Mankind
Punctuality	Courage	Cunning	Thrift	Faith in Law / Suppression of Fear and Pain
Regularity of Life / System	Sincerity / Generosity	Envy / Anger	Abstinence / Conscience	The Square Deal / Social Responsibility / Devotion to Democratic Ideals
Endurance / Prudence / Temperance	Charity / Good-will / Gentleness	Revenge / Gossip / Jealousy	Contentment / Belief in Self-help / The Sacredness of Agreements / Total Abstinence	
Reliability	Fairness	Meanness	The Seclusion of Women	The Elevation of Woman / Missionary Zeal
Truthfulness	Trust	Vanity		
Honesty / Cleanliness / Cheerfulness	Sympathy / Patriotism / Love of Home	Lawlessness / Laziness / Superstition	Sunday Observance / Loyalty to Conviction / Restriction of Hours of Labor / Prohibition of Child Labor / The Safeguarding of Labor / The Closed Shop	The Open Shop / Racial Equality / Revolt Against Sweatshop Products / Tenement-house Reform / Public Sanitation
Obedience	Mutual Aid	Gambling		
Love of Work	Neighborliness	Prostitution		
Self-control	Love of Festivals	Dissipation		
Team-work	Sensitiveness to Pain	Prejudice	Belief in Providence	The Extension of Civilization / Belief in Social Redemption
Pleasure in Work	Social Approval	Cruelty	Social Solidarity	Civic Cooperation

CHAPTER IX

THE NEW CIVILIZATION

CHAPTER IX

THE NEW CIVILIZATION

GOOD times have been so often overthrown by calamity that men scarcely trust their senses when evidences of prosperity confront them. Conservatism hurls charges of optimism and impracticability at those who admit they are cheered by present indications and takes little heed of the doleful tales and vague fears of current lore. Men reason as though it were normal to despond, and weak to color one's opinions with a vigorous independence. A doubting habit of mind affects even those who see within the dim future the unfolding of a new civilization, and who dwell upon the ills of the present in order to brighten the glories of some distant day. It is difficult to make vivid the picture of the civilization we might now enjoy side by side with the glorious vision of the ideal civilization drawn by the perfectionists. An ideal civilization is not a twentieth-century possibility. A thousand, perhaps many thousand, years must elapse before the multitude of material adjustments necessary to it will have been completed. In the meantime, society must either rest upon its old bases or else refashion itself out of the knowledge and resources within the environment at any given time. A higher civilization is a present possibility that may be realized by people living in this century. It is ready now to appear; but its emergence implies a change of opinions, ideals, and institutions, and a shifting from past to present conditions. And there must be no halt for more information, skill, or racial aptness.

Disease, oppression, irregular work, premature old age, and race hatreds characterized the vanishing age of deficit; plenty of food, shelter, capital, security, and mobility of men and goods define the age of surplus in which we act. Where food and capital are, there is work, and where there is steady work, progress comes even while wages remain low. The quantities of food and of capital will increase more rapidly than they have done, while the birth-rate touches a lower figure in every census. Population once pressed hard upon food and employment; now food is ready for consumers and capital calls for workers. Many occupations and many localities are hampered by a "labor famine" — a famine which will spread as harvests multiply and capital expands. It would already have been more seriously felt had the dearth not been concealed by a tremendous immigration, an extended employment of women and children, and the greater regularity of work. The regularity of work and women in industry have added to the family goods, even though they retard the advance of wages measured by the hour and day. But the shortening of hours, the exclusion of children from industry, and the raising of the home standard will check further increase of labor force in these directions. The demand for more workers must then be met by more families. Immigration has supplied them hitherto; but there are definite limits to that source of increase. Large surplus populations come now only from Austria, Italy, and Russia, countries which in a few generations will be drained as North Europe has been. Assuming that the white race will control and people the parts of the earth it now holds, population will be redistributed so evenly before the end of the century that the nations must supply their own labor markets. Then the swelling supplies of food and capital will effect themselves naturally, and the rate of wages will rise.

The salient feature of the new civilization is work calling urgently for workmen; that of the old was the worker seeking humbly any kind of toil. To recall fleetingly how the lack of work has crushed and cowed men; how social traditions are formed on the existence of a servile class; how the scarcity of food and the fear of want have shadowed the buoyant spirits of the poor and have bred race hatreds — to recall these things is to realize in part how fundamentally this one change will affect many familiar landmarks. The new civilization means a self-reliant workman with freedom of thought and mobility of movement. It means the regulation and assurance of industry, and the worker squarely established in his environment, because he has become courageous enough to make use of what he already knows and to fit his acts to his situation. One chapter alone in history is comparable with the results which full economic freedom will bring about; political liberty has affected the institutions and ideals of nations as economic equality will after a shorter lapse of time.

But the tendencies of progress and of long static poverty are in opposition, and are divided by a line above which men possess energy, vigor, and efficiency, and from which their families move upward generation after generation by steps not hard to climb. Below the line disease, want, dissipation, and superstition seize and hold their victims with a tightening grasp. If they were annihilated, we could console ourselves that out of the evil good comes. But the weak multiply fastest when they suffer most, and greater numbers are born to take the place of those who fall beneath poverty. The more rapidly the gaps in the ranks are filled, the more strongly does misery intrench itself. The men of poverty may be uplifted under new social standards, but the class cannot be eliminated by its suffering.

The dividing line between progress and degeneration is not identical with that which marks a people's standard of life; it is the line of release from the full dominion of poverty, and from it men can advance to a natural standard which is the measure of the successful endeavors, the substantial gains, and the habits and comforts that the prosperous members of the race enjoy. The standard of life may be high at a time when the poverty class, arrested by its wretchedness, is not only static, but is deteriorating; so that the acquired happiness upon one level may be in inverse ratio to the mean of suffering upon the other. We can find the point at which degeneration begins, for it is fixed by physical agencies the force and direction of which may be readily determined. We know in a general way how much of the suffering of the poor comes from disease. We must also estimate how much arises from the shortening of adult life by toil and from the length of the working day.

A widespread cause of the unhappiness of the poor is the lessening term of the working life, which brings it about that the older generation cannot hold out until the younger is able to take its place. The burdens of child-bearing and early rearing fall chiefly between the ages of twenty-five and forty; since fifteen more years elapse before the youngest child reaches the working age, the period of thirty years is the minimum time necessary for the maturing of each generation. Unless the working life of the parents is equally long, the laborer does not escape the grasp of want. A short-lived race must suffer the familiar woes of poverty; but in it also develop the gambler's spirit, a disregard for life, an indifference toward pain, a desire to take risks, and a craving for dissipation. The root of these evils is reached when the working day is shortened and life is lengthened to permit the worker who is forced to be impulsive and careless to become a cautious producer for future needs. Morality and restrictive legislation cannot do what these two deeds of social justice can, in creating motives that raise men from despondent shift-lessness to alert efficiency. Ten hours of sedentary routine in crowded rooms, or of hard manual work that offers no perspectives to the mind, stupefy the laborer and drain the force that ought to be stored for to-morrow. Whoever has seen such a toiler after he has slipped from the harness, saturated with fatigue, dozing heavily in a chair or urging his faculties more actively by recourse to the excitements of the streets, knows that no profits can overcome the losses of the long day. The death-rate of workers between the ages of twenty-five and fifty-five also strongly hinders progress, because death removes the chief support of a family. At present one-third of the men die between those years. Many of the survivors are incapacitated long before they reach the half-century line, and the lives of laborers are much shorter than the terms of other men. If to these evils we add the misery due to the lack of work and other misfortunes, it seems inevitable that at least one family in four must experience the repressions of poverty long enough to undergo physical deterioration and to receive lasting impressions upon their opinions, their imagination, and their emotions.

One-half of this mortality is already preventable. It may be attributed either to accidents which need not have occurred, to diseases arising from bad sanitation, or to dissipation, poor food, and ignorance. These conditions are in sharp contrast with those we might have if existing knowledge were utilized for the relief of the workers. A comparison of the records of illness and death among American soldiers in the Spanish War with those of the Japanese during their war with Russia shows that our methods of handling disease are wastefully careless, and that theirs are truly scientific. In our armies there were fourteen deaths from disease to one from wounds, and more than 95 per cent of those from disease were traced to neglected hygiene. They were therefore needless losses. In the Japanese armies there was one death from disease to four from wounds. The Japanese have a lively appreciation of the value of a life as an asset in war and in commerce. If Americans would realize the value of laborers in an industrial civilization, they could conserve as the Japanese do. On any count, the laborer is worth more than the soldier, of whom the state takes better care because it is cheaper to keep him alive after paying the cost of moving him to the front than it is to replace him. It is sheer carelessness that lets the laborer die. We do not think one life matters much, for another man is ready to step into the vacant place, and the social philosophy in which we are schooled teaches that people have always struggled with each other for food, and that one man's death makes place for another who else could not have lived. When we estimate life at its potential uses, all this will be changed, and the rate will fall toward that touched by Japan when a national crisis forced her to set a just value upon her men.

Renewed emphasis is thus laid upon the part of general well-being that must be secured through social coöperation. Health can be improved and education extended only by means beyond the reach of individuals.

They are properly in the budget of the nation, and should not be added to that of the family. Society fixes the conditions of healthfulness in a community; the family secures food, pays rent, and meets the costs of rearing children. The contrast of the income of families with health-making conditions given by the community is a test of the efficiency of private and public efforts. The comparison shows that the family is less to blame than the community when it falls below the line of poverty, for its degeneration seems to be due to the failure of the public to insure healthful conditions to the family. The present relation of income to wants may be seen more clearly in the case of single men and women than in that of families. In the life of both sexes there is a lengthening period between the beginning of the working years and the marriageable age, when the standards of the individuals are directly made by their income. Whatever they are, they are carried into marriage; if the first epoch is one of advance, the second is likely to be also. The mobility, the freedom of choice, and the courage gained by the young workers will ultimately readjust their situation so that they will be able as families to keep what they won alone. Observation shows that men cross the threshold of this economic release when they are sure of earning ten dollars a week, and that women do when they have

o [193]

steady work at seven dollars. With these regular incomes they have the satisfying assurance that they can be comfortably housed, amply fed, and recreated by the amusements that give zest to life. Add the two sums together, and there is an annual income of eight hundred dollars, a budget which will maintain a family above the line of poverty. But so easy a transition is arrested by the social tradition that excludes young wives from industry. Once the household industries gave to the home-staying woman a fair share of the labor, but to-day they are few, and the "home-maker" suffers under enforced idleness, ungratified longing, and non-productive time-killing. Family standards must remain low when the full labor power of the whole unit is not freed; and the consequent loss of energy in such a case often makes us forget how much the courage, vigor, and zeal of women are worth to the race. Heredity has not been making idleness good for women while it has been making work good for men. Valuable qualities are developed by toil, and women improve as men do under its discipline and rewards. And, moreover, it is not necessary that all women should be employed outside the home in order to insure an income of eight hundred dollars. If twenty-five is the normal age of marriage, one-quarter of the working population — that between fifteen and twenty-five — is unmarried, and about one of every ten above that year will probably remain single or will have no children. The number of families approximates one-third of the number of workers, and there are three workers in each family group. The earnings of the third member — a relative, a boarder, or a lodger — ought to be the pension that honorably retires the mother from industry during the child-bearing decades. But the new social situation does demand that the opposition to women in industry shall disappear, for no standards of civilization can be raised without their active and concerted coöperation.

Mr. Hoffman[1] computes society's economic gain through an efficient worker according to the value of the product over and above the wages paid, the costs of supervision and materials, and the miscellaneous expenses of the plant. By this estimate the average workman is worth $200. But the valuation is far too low. Each new family adds to the rental of land, increases the profits of the trades, and broadens the opportunities to invest capital. Every class, trade, and profession is in a definite numerical relation to the group of basal workers, and grows as it grows. Double the number of workers in a city, and the number of

[1] "Physical and Medical Aspects of Labor and Industry," Annals of American Academy of Political and Social Science, May, 1906.

men in the various pursuits will be multiplied, land will become more than twice as valuable, and profits will swell still more rapidly. Therefore it is moderate to assert that a family which earns $500 a year for itself will add an equal sum to the income of the classes above it. Sickness, death, or loss of employment in a laborer's family means spiritual and physical misery; loss of income by the other classes follows the withdrawal of the workman from industry. The family disrupted by such disasters cannot bear the cost of preventing them. Only the classes whose incomes enlarge proportionally with the growth of population can or ought to pay the costs. Surely, if society is yearly richer by $500 through the activity of a family, it is not too much to say that one-tenth of the sum should be spent to keep it in good health. One-tenth is not a high replacement cost for fixed capital; cannot society pay as much to replace one generation with another, which shall surpass it in body and mind as the new tool and building surpass the old in excellence?

Education was socialized when men began to perceive its returns in efficiency and good citizenship. Industry will be socialized and poverty checked when health and energy are given their due consideration. Then a park will be made beside every schoolhouse, all water will be as pure as that flowing from a spring, light and air will be as clear in the city as they are in the mountains, and the street will be as clean and safe and honest as the home. Uncertain health is a potent cause of weak character. Neither productive power nor riches nor cheapened commodities can give the workers the normal stimuli of character-building until they have been given good housing, elaborate sanitation, shorter hours of work, protection from disease, and the tempered life that these imply. Health is a matter of nutrition, not of heredity. Four out of five children are born with normal senses and a vigor that promises sound and rapid growth. It is the environment of the children of the poor that inflates the death-rate and dwarfs them below the stature of a man.

There can be no permanent progress until poverty has been eliminated, for then only will the normally evolving man, dominant through numbers and keen mental powers, force adjustments, generation by generation, which will raise the general level of intellect and character. And when poverty is gone, the last formidable obstacle to the upward movement of the race will have disappeared. Our children's children may learn with amazement how we thought it a natural social phenomenon that men should die in their prime, leaving wives and children in terror of want; that accidents should make an army of maimed dependents; that there should not be enough houses for workers; and that epidemics should sweep away multitudes as autumn frost sweeps away summer insects. They will wonder that the universal sadness of such a world should have appealed to our transient sympathies but did not absorb our widest interests. They will ask why there was some hope of succor for those whose miseries passed for a moment before the eyes of the tender-hearted, but none for the dwellers beyond the narrow horizon within which pity moves. And they will be unable to put themselves in our places, because the new social philosophy which we are this moment framing will have so moulded their minds that they cannot return to the philosophy that moulds ours.

It is for us to unite the social activities — whose motive forces are charity, religion, philanthropy, revolt, and unrest — into a philosophy that is social and not sectional, in that it gives to them all a reorganized rational body of evidence upon which to proceed. They will then understand each other while doing the work that transforms the world into a place worth living in. It was a perception that to sympathy and charitable impulse must be added knowledge and skill which founded the school of philanthropy. If the social worker would be a social philosopher and the reformer a builder as well as a destroyer, he must know how to use the matter and the spirit that make the philanthropies, the trades unions, the settlements, the institutional churches, and the theatres. Economists groping among the formulæ of deficit are surprised and overtaken by the new world, and statesmen are bewildered by the surge of the new democracy of industrial liberty against the barriers of class. But these difficulties only prove that the new civilization will be ready as soon as social work has been made a science and is practised with knowledge and ideals which make clear to the statesman who directs and the workman who produces the treasures in health and happiness and safety of the new time.

CHAPTER X

A PROGRAMME OF SOCIAL WORK

CHAPTER X

A PROGRAMME OF SOCIAL WORK

THERE still continues, I fear, a feeling of impatience on the part of social workers with the philosophy that lies at the basis of their activities. The books they read or the lectures they hear start out well and often kindle a real enthusiasm, but in the end they leave the confused worker in a quagmire of contradictions far from the points of real interest. The hearer may have had a pleasant evening, but the morning dawns with no new light on the work of the day. Can the pleasure of the evening be transformed into enthusiasm for work? Is there any relation between thought and practice? A social philosophy should furnish a hand-book that might be on the desk of every worker, however humble, and from which might be drawn the principles and examples that fit the work of the day. Is this true or can it be made true of the newer social philosophy that is just beginning to gain expounders? The impulses of the thinker are the same as those that inspire the worker, and the environment he studies coincides with that within which the worker toils. The gulf between them need not exist. It will cease when the thought of to-day is so stated that the worker may comprehend it. This however is no light task, but it is worth a trial even if it fails.

The striking aspect of the recent development of thought is the changing concept concerning the part heredity plays in life. Men have been trained from the earliest times to attach great importance to the influence of blood descent upon racial and individual character. Some families and peoples are said to be inherently superior to others, because they have possessed, generation after generation, well-marked qualities which others did not have. The differences between them were readily explained by heredity, so readily, in fact, that more influence was soon given to ancestry than to the environment into which a man was born. This unequal division of power seems to be destroyed by recent discoveries in biology, which are establishing a new equilibrium between natural or inherited qualities and those acquired after birth. Many qualities are inherited, but the number is smaller than it was thought to be, and many of them may be readily suppressed by the action of the environment in which men live, so that they do not show themselves for long periods in a particular family or a given race. This curtailment of the force of physical heredity gives more power to the acquired qualities handed on from generation to generation as a social tradition. A physical inheritance, simpler than we thought, is ours at birth; but there is a larger and increasingly important social heredity which must be constantly renewed through the conscious efforts of parents and teachers.

The recognition of man's power over heredity is equalled by the perception of his power over nature as it is shown by his achievements in industry. Food is abundant, income grows, and machines do the old drudgeries. That work is pleasant, the environment is good, and human nature is a group of ennobling qualities are now axioms that contrast the new thought with the old philosophy of deficit so long taught and so ardently defended. The depraved man is not the natural man; for in him the natural is suppressed beneath a crushing load of misfortunes, superstitions, and ill-fitting social conventions. But in spite of the good hope that follows, elation is replaced by dejection as soon as we remember that poverty is scarcely mitigated by prosperity. The normal qualities of human nature are modified so slowly and under such complex conditions that the reformer often believes himself helpless to make the improvements he longs for. The biologists do not encourage him, if he looks to them for help, for they say it is a matter of ages to engraft a new characteristic upon humanity. If this indeed is true we can create neither virtues nor heroes nor genius. We can be no more than watchers of changes as slow and inevitable as the subsidences and elevations of the earth's surfaces.

Now look at the brighter side. It is, without doubt, more difficult than was once believed to lift a man with normal faculties to a higher plane of existence; but it is far easier than we have thought to raise a man below the general level of humanity up to it. There are no differences between him and his normal neighbors which cannot be rapidly obliterated. He does not lack their blood, but their health, their vigor, their good fortune, their culture, and their environment. The doctrine which teaches that evolution is the slowest of moving forces also teaches that the distinctions between men on the two sides of the line of poverty are frailer than we have been led to believe. The faculties and social qualities of human nature were implanted in it before the beginnings of history; but health, vigor, and good fortune are determined by to-day's environment. Poverty is not rooted in a debased heredity nor in a world-wide lack of work. The motives of the unfortunate have weakened while the inclinations of standard men to labor have remained strong enough to lead them to efficient activity. The men in whom energy is sapped, or who have been the victims of misfortune, are a class in which the normal race stimuli are failing to act. The loaf of bread, the cigar, the theatre ticket held before men as rewards to work re-main inducements only until they have been consumed. Zeal wanes as they are used up, and will not steadily flow again except from a fund of surplus energy that in its exit sharpens imagination and revives the drooping faculties. Give rain and crops grow; give surplus energy and men become spontaneously efficient. Land is the slow accumulations of past ages as the faculties of men are the sum of the slow changes in heredity. Both are what the past has bequeathed, and both are useless unless vitalized by material within the present. Rain is a small part of the aggregate of conditions upon which crops depend, but all the others are valueless in drought. And so is energy a small fraction of the powers of nor-mal man; lacking it, however, his manifold faculties fail to function. The depletion of energy, induced and aggravated by misfortunes, is the crucial distinction between poverty and normal men. Upon the heels of misfortune follow superstitions and ill-fitting social conventions, which intensify growing differences by the mental habits they entail. And thus it comes about that differences which at bottom are wholly objective

NEW BASIS OF CIVILIZATION

form peculiarities in thought that seem to denote a specialized mental heredity in the more fortunate of the race. But health, vigor, and right conditions would soon change all this, and race types would fade with the differences between environments and the quantities of energy within them. When sanitation, good housing, and shorter hours of work have generated enough energy to release starving faculties, poverty men will adjust themselves as capably as normal men and will also appreciate culture and morality. Poverty men are primitive men cowed by hardships, and they must be encouraged by methods that stir primitive people to deeds that seem to be heroic and marvellous. The opportunity to perform thrilling and dramatic feats is taken wherever accidents happen and the lazy or incapable passer-by is transformed into an eager worker. Of such a sort was an habitual vagrant who, having persistently refused offers of work and evaded his family responsibilities, was being taken to court by an officer, when flames burst through the windows of a house they were passing. He broke away from the policeman, dashed into the blinding smoke, and came out half carrying two stupefied women. He then returned to the officer and went on to receive a loafer's punishment. Which was the fundamental man, the laggard in work or the hero in a life-and-death struggle?

He had "bad habits," but far deeper in him lay noble instincts and swift, accurate reactions to duties which he understood. In common with most men, he was instantly responsive and energetic in a sudden interesting situation. But the indirect action, the round-about methods of the industrial world, did not stimulate. The imagination that vivifies remote deeds and makes their rewards worth while is feeble in men depleted by physical losses or untrained in industrial methods which necessitate application and foresight. A dramatic summons is worth more than hours of advice to the unawakened man.

A girl of the streets who had adopted crime as a profession, because life in a ribbon factory did not interest her, was committed to a reformatory and assigned to active labor in the gardens and grounds. Her enjoyment of it was keen, and her work so excellent that she soon became boss of an out-of-door squad. At the end of her term she said that there was no use of being "bad" now that she had a chance to live in the country and do the things she had always wanted to do. Which is the real woman, the vicious prostitute or the bright worker rising on the first opportunity to become efficient? What shall we say of the governor who vetoed an appropriation which would have built hot-houses where the market demand for gardeners could have

NEW BASIS OF CIVILIZATION

been supplied from trained prisoners? Is he right in
believing that bad girls are always bad and that their
restoration to health and safe surroundings by training
them to meet the demand for employees was not an
economy to a great state?

The poor are not alone in the search for vivid inducements to be active. The leisure class stimulates its
vitality by amusements fetched from far and near.
Hunting, racing, dancing, banqueting, and the exercise
of power are direct excitements which make them
energetic. Danger and dissipation move them as their
ancestors were moved when they fought hand to hand
with animals and men. The perilous speed of an auto-
mobile arouses strong emotions that normal life fails
to waken. These emotions, expressed through pleasure
by the well-to-do, are such as poverty men need to make
them work with enjoyment. It is as necessary to
educate the rich to an appreciation of indirect distant
gratifications as it is to teach the poor to understand
the values in work at more than one remove from the
object of desire. Efficiency is indirect work; generosity
is indirect enjoyment. Both are stages in the same
process of reviving the imagination so that it arouses
action and emotion. A rich man who never gives is
as abnormal as the poor man who never works. The
shell of self-interest has never been pierced by a shaft

strong enough to free the flood of sympathy and good-will beneath it. And most forms of organized phi-lanthropy, religion, and education fail to sink that shaft because they do not use vivid methods of appeal to indifferent men. The public is moved to give money to a hospital because the rush of the ambulance betokens swift, full rescue from disaster or death. But a char-itable society too often seems to delay aid until it shall have filled its schedules of investigations. The man in the street is only touched to quick pity and generosity by dramatic appeal for the succor of victims of earth-quake, disease, fire, and horrible accident. The road from this spasmodic giving to steady systematic relief aimed at the sources of poverty must be brightened by flashlight pictures of charitable work done as promptly as an ambulance corps does its work on a battlefield. Society needs more emotion and clearer motive rather than more income with which to regenerate itself.

It therefore becomes the social worker's first task to discover how faculties may be made active, how industry may be stimulated, and how men may be surrounded — rich and poor alike — with conditions that shall renew energy and after every expenditure of it bring it back greater than it went out. The measure of increase is the freshness of imagination and the keenness of motive. There is, moreover, another task of equal magnitude.

The social worker must examine himself to learn whether or no his own motives and emotions are powerful enough to break the traditions that bind him. Does not he also neglect the distant good, and treat superficial symptoms of disorder? And, most futile attempt of all, does he not struggle to create new traits and to construct new social conventions when he should be striving to make men free by removing the pressure that stifles feeling and disintegrates motive? Let us have more confidence in what nature has implanted in heredity and less in what we as individuals can add to it. Our own forms of culture, our own religion, and our own system of morality seem to be the embodiment of fixed ideals which alone can lift men above the common-place level of their fellows. Therefore we are urgent in transferring this body of practice to the poor in the hope that it will affect their lives as it has ours. But have we first aroused the imagination and trained it so that these ideals will attract and hold them? Have they the energy, functioning in a proper environment, which will start them toward remote rewards that are not at the moment very desirable? The means of progress are material; its ends are ideal. We will reach the ends only when we lose sight of them in the struggle for material improvements.

The truth of this is partially seen by social workers,

but they do not yet see as clearly as they should the distinction between the regeneration of the poverty class and the progress of normal men. The aim of social work is democracy rather than culture; energy rather than virtue; health rather than income; efficiency rather than goodness; and social standards for all rather than genius and opportunity for the few. It may be shocking to put these contrasts so forcefully; I do it, not to depreciate the old ideals closely associated with progress, but to make emphatic the means by which they are reached. In whatever direction progress may seem to lie, an ideal has been erected as the prize to be striven for which shines forth in our thoughts; but the means of reaching it are not also made vivid. And therefore we honor the herculean toilers who strive to cut direct roads toward the goal of the ideal. We encourage self-denial when we should encourage self-expression. We try to suppress vices when we should release virtues. We laud country life when we should strive for the improvement of cities. We judge the poor by their family history when we should judge them by their latent powers. We impose penalties when we should offer rewards. We ask for the gratitude of the poor when we ought to point out their rights to them. We dwell too long upon the weaknesses of the man who drinks and too little upon why the saloon remains at the corner. Too heavy stress is laid on the duties of parents to children and too little upon the obligations of teachers, authors, editors, and doctors, who do, in fact, exercise a stronger influence on the health and character of a city child than its parents can. We also over-estimate the power of the home to mould its members, and in consequence neglect to utilize the institutions of city life. We rely on restraint to shape the characters of boys when we should be thinking of their recreations. As the city home becomes smaller its unity is interfered with. The functions it loses are taken over by the growing town, and in their exercise is to be found the process of character making which was carried on in the older form of the isolated home. The farmer knew his farm on which his sons grew up; the wife knew the house, yard, and garden in which her daughters carried on their varied industries. Father and mother were then the natural guides. But now they may never see the parts of the city in which their children work or know of their amusements and temptations. Social workers should idealize and purify the city for this new occupation by the young as the moralists have long sought to preserve the safety of the home. In this transitional period we cannot expect as much aid from the church and Sunday-school as from the newspaper and the political party. They are the agencies by which

A PROGRAMME OF SOCIAL WORK

men transform local abuses into justice and through
which men secure the reforms for which they ask.

Character is acquired by example, not by blood; by
the activities and amusements in the shop and street,
not by the restraints of church and home. The new
morality does not consist in saving, but in expanding
consumption; not in draining men of their energy, but in
storing up a surplus in the weak and young; not in the
process of hardening, but in extending the period of
recreation and leisure; not in the thought of the future,
but in the utilization and expansion of the present. We
lack efficiency, not capital; pleasures, not goods; keen
present interests, not solemn warnings of future woes;
courage to live joyous lives, not remorse, sacrifice, and renunciation. The morality of restraint comes later than
the morality of activity; for men need restraint only
after poverty disappears. And hence we must return
with renewed emphasis to the thought that social work
has to do with the means of progress and not with its
ends. But the ideals of progress have become so incorporated into our thought that we instinctively place
them in the foreground and neglect the activity which
must open the way to them.

Progress in thought is obtained by a change from conventional standards to ideal standards. Conventions
are a weight that the distant past has placed on us.

NEW BASIS OF CIVILIZATION

Ideals project us into an equally distant future. There are ideals but no ideal activities, because the ideal is thought projected into the future while activity is in the present and must always go out toward the next thing, not toward the distant thing. Activities are either self-centred or social. We can have a selfish programme or we can have a social programme, but we cannot have an ideal programme; for programmes relate to activities and not to thought. "Hitch your wagon to a star" is a great thought well expressed, but no one can work out a programme by which it can be done. We often see well-deserving movements start out with flying banners, happy phrases, and great enthusiasm, only to find the road to the stars blocked at the first hill-side. To be effective ideal constructive thought must be transferred into practical social work, and hence the need of the contrast between ideal ends and the indirect means by which they are reached. Many illustrations might be given, but I content myself with a table in which some of these contrasts are given and by which one may judge of his natural inclinations and the cogency of my criticisms.

A PROGRAMME OF SOCIAL WORK

ENDS	THE INDIRECT MEANS
National Prosperity	Health
Income	Energy
Culture	Democracy
Art	Pleasurable Work
Ideals	Habits
Goodness	Efficiency
Admiration of Power	Admiration of Results
Restraint	Recreation
Character	Social Control
Saving	Generosity
Service-altruism	Income-altruism
Temperance	Diet
Self-denial	Self-expression
Obedience	Independence
Home	City Life
Woman's Purity	Woman's Ability
Support of Women	Their Work and Energy
History of Failures	Chart of Capacity

A chart like the foregoing helps to classify the different kinds of social endeavor and to distinguish the field of the social worker from those of the moralist, the artist, the idealist, and other advocates of higher standards. The social worker prepares the ground, pulls the weeds, and builds shelter for the weak. The idealists tend the flowers, cultivate the tender fruits, and erect delicate buildings to house art, pleasure, and worship. Democracy wins for the masses what evolution and struggle has given to the few. Do you desire the evolution of character? Would you help to create new and higher virtues? Are you more zealous for new forms of art than for the spread of what we have? Do you believe that progress comes through genius and heroes or through many slight improvements in the lot of the multitudes? Then progress and culture is your goal, and you should strive for them by direct means. But if you acknowledge kinship with the masses, have faith in humanity and would strive for its elevation, regeneration should be your watchword, and you should promote the interests of the weak rather than to give nurture to the strong. When a social worker accepts this creed and no longer searches for superman, he soon finds that regeneration is prevented not by defects in personality, but by defects in the environment, and that the subjective tests of character to which he has been accustomed must be replaced by objective standards which test the environment. We need not work for regeneration; it will of itself flow from sources we neither create nor control. But we do need to work for the removal of external conditions, which by suppressing and distorting human nature give to vice the power that virtue should possess.

I have laid stress on the self-examination that the social worker should impose on himself. I want to

A PROGRAMME OF SOCIAL WORK

make it equally emphatic that no such test should be applied to poverty men. Their motives, their vices, and their family history should not be made prominent in the tests applied to them. They are what they are because of their situation, which gives them no opportunity to express their inherent but suppressed qualities. We must establish objective standards of efficiency of energy and of living drawn from those who have been released from poverty. It is not necessary to measure the differences in character and virtue between normal men and those on the verge of poverty; it is enough to determine the differences in environment and in the social standards surrounding these two classes. The virtues, the powers, and the energies of the poor will approximate those of the prosperous when the conditions and social standards of the two classes are the same. We must go beyond the tests of personality and family so often employed and set up the standard of each locality as the norm by which the defects and shortcomings of the poor are to be measured. Without such standards social workers cannot determine how much of the poverty about them is due to the ignorance and inefficiency of the poor, and how much to exploitation by their employers; nor can they fix by the responsibility of the state in caring for the health and welfare of its citizens. What wages must a workman have in

NEW BASIS OF CIVILIZATION

order to be a happy, useful member of his community, and what must the state contribute to this end? These are not vague questions to be answered by some preconceived theory; they demand an actual investigation in each locality and city — which should take precedence over all inquiries into problems of relief, sympathy, or betterment, for no relief or betterment is effective that leaves the person aided below the standard of his fellows. Each social movement should be measured by the number of independent self-supporting families it makes. A failure to reach this objective end means a failure everywhere, for the work must be done again and again until the advantages of independence and efficiency are reached. Nor is it so difficult as it seems to measure the standard of living in a locality; it requires merely a transference of interest from the history and lives of the poor to their environment, their food, and their work. A case is not completely recorded by the account of their failures and woes. Back of them is the crushing force of those external conditions which should be on our schedules even more fully than the items of personal history and misfortune. Measure the conditions of the poor objectively and relieve them fully. Only thus will poverty disappear and democracy be created in which every one is independent and free.

THE JOHN HARVARD LIBRARY

The intent of
Waldron Phoenix Belknap, Jr.,
as expressed in an early will, was for
Harvard College to use the income from a
permanent trust fund he set up, for "editing and
publishing rare, inaccessible, or hitherto unpublished
source material of interest in connection with the
history, literature, art (including minor and useful
art), commerce, customs, and manners or way of
life of the Colonial and Federal Periods of the United
States . . . In all cases the emphasis shall be on the
presentation of the basic material." A later testament
broadened this statement, but Mr. Belknap's interests remained constant until his death.
    In linking the name of the first benefactor of
Harvard College with the purpose of this later,
generous-minded believer in American culture the
John Harvard Library seeks to emphasize the importance of Mr. Belknap's purpose. The John Harvard
Library of the Belknap Press of Harvard University
Press exists to make books and documents
about the American past more readily
available to scholars and the
general reader.